UFOs

Fact or Fiction?

Terry O'Neill, *Book Editor*

Daniel Leone, *President*
Bonnie Szumski, *Publisher*
Scott Barbour, *Managing Editor*

OPPOSING
VIEWPOINTS®
SERIES

Greenhaven
Press®

THOMSON
———✱———™
GALE

San Diego • Detroit • New York • San Francisco • Cleveland
New Haven, Conn. • Waterville, Maine • London • Munich

YA
001.942
UFO
c.1

LIBRARY OF CONGRESS CATALOGING-IN-PUBLICATION DATA

O'Neill, Terry, 1944–
UFOs / Terry O'Neill, book editor.
    p. cm. — (Fact or fiction?)
Includes bibliographical references and index.
ISBN 0-7377-1069-1 (pbk. : alk. paper) —
ISBN 0-7377-1070-5 (hardback : alk. paper)
    1. Unidentified flying objects—Juvenile literature. [1. Unidentified flying objects.] I. Title. II. Fact or fiction? (Greenhaven Press)

TL789.2 O54   2003
001.942—dc21   2002000498

Printed in the United States of America

Contents

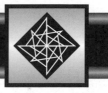

Foreword   5
Introduction   7

Chapter 1: UFOs Are Fact
1. Flying Saucers Are Real   23
   Kenneth J. Arnold

2. A UFO Crashed Near Roswell, New Mexico   30
   Charles Berlitz and Willliam L. Moore

3. Evidence: Physical Traces in France   38
   Don Berliner with Marie Galbraith and
   Antonio Huneeus

4. Evidence: Radar and Visual Sighting in Tehran   46
   Lawrence Fawcett and Barry J. Greenwood

5. Evidence: Military Eyewitnesses in England   55
   Michael Hesemann

6. The Government Is Hiding UFO Evidence   65
   Lynn Picknett

Chapter 2: UFOs Are Fiction
1. Evidence of UFOs Is Insufficient   75
   Edward U. Condon

2. Explanation: Research Balloons and Dummies   81
   James McAndrew

3. Explanation: Natural Earthlights   95
   Paul Devereux

4. Explanation: Venus   106
   Bob Berman

5. Explanation: Delusion   111
   Robert L. Park

6. Explanation: Experimental Aircraft   117
   Jim Wilson

7. The Media Irresponsibly Encourage Belief
   in UFOs   122
   Art Levine

8. I Want Proof   126
   Alan Hale

Epilogue: Analyzing the Evidence   131
For Further Research   152
Index   156

Foreword

"There are more things in heaven and earth, Horatio, than are dreamt of in your philosophy."
—William Shakespeare, *Hamlet*

"Extraordinary claims require extraordinary evidence."
—Carl Sagan, *The Demon-Haunted World*

Almost every one of us has experienced something that we thought seemed mysterious and unexplainable. For example, have you ever known that someone was going to call you just before the phone rang? Or perhaps you have had a dream about something that later came true. Some people think these occurrences are signs of the paranormal. Others explain them as merely coincidence.

As the examples above show, mysteries of the paranormal ("beyond the normal") are common. For example, most towns have at least one place where inhabitants believe ghosts live. People report seeing strange lights in the sky that they believe are the spaceships of visitors from other planets. And scientists have been working for decades to discover the truth about sightings of mysterious creatures like Bigfoot and the Loch Ness monster.

There are also mysteries of magic and miracles. The two often share a connection. Many forms of magical belief are tied to religious belief. For example, many of the rituals and beliefs of the voodoo religion are viewed by outsiders as magical practices. These include such things as the alleged Haitian voodoo practice of turning people into zombies (the walking dead).

There are mysteries of history—events and places that have been recorded in history but that we still have questions about today. For example, was the great King Arthur a real king or merely a legend? How, exactly, were the pyramids built? Historians continue to seek the answers to these questions. Then, of course, there are mysteries of science. One such mystery is how humanity began. Although most scientists agree that it was through the long, slow process of evolution, not all scientists agree that indisputable proof has been found.

Subjects like these are fascinating, in part because we do not know the whole truth about them. They are mysteries. And they are controversial—people hold very strong and opposing views about them.

How we go about sifting through information on such topics is the subject of every book in the Greenhaven Press series Fact or Fiction? Each anthology includes articles that present the main ideas favoring and challenging a given topic. The editor collects such material from a variety of sources, including scientific research, eyewitness accounts, and government reports. In addition, a final chapter gives readers tools to analyze the articles they read. With these tools, readers can sift through the information presented in the articles by applying the methods of hypothetical reasoning. Examining these topics in this way adds a unique aspect to the Fact or Fiction? series. Hypothetical reasoning can be applied to any topic to allow a reader to become more analytical about the material he or she encounters. While such reasoning may not solve the mystery of who is right or who is wrong, it can help the reader separate valid from invalid evidence relating to all topics and can be especially helpful in analyzing material where people disagree.

Introduction

"And I looked, and, behold, a whirlwind came out of the north, a great cloud, and a fire infolding itself, and a brightness *was* about it, and out of the midst thereof as the colour of amber, out of the midst of the fire.

"Also out of the midst therof *came* the likeness of four living creatures. And this *was* their appearance; they had the likeness of a man."

Bible, Book of Ezekiel, 1:4–5, King James version

Did Ezekiel, the biblical prophet, see a UFO? Some UFO believers say that the passage above is just one piece of evidence that UFOs have been witnessed by humans for eons. Other believers point to the traditional stories told in most cultures about visitors from the heavens and to images in ancient art that seem to show spaceships flying in the medieval sky and space-suited astronauts populating Mayan tombs and ancient Japanese statuary. Those who see UFOs in these stories and images point out that people today who claim to see UFOs are not seeing something unusual; the space visitors have been with us throughout human civilization. But others say the ancient images are not depicting UFOs at all. Rather, they say, we have imposed modern ideas onto ancient art and artifacts.

While ancient evidence may be open to interpretation, certainly many people in modern times have unambiguously reported seeing things that they believe are UFOs. And many others who have not seen a UFO themselves believe they exist. Astronaut Eugene Cernan, *Apollo 17* commander, told the *Los Angeles Times*, "I'm one of those guys that have never seen a UFO. But I've been asked, and I've said publicly I thought they were somebody else; some other civilization."[1] Cernan is not alone. In fact, a May 2001 poll conducted by a major research organization, the Gallup Organization, shows that 33 percent of Americans believe "that extraterrestrial beings have visited earth at some time in the past."[2] A 1996 poll by the same organization showed that 12 percent believed they had actually seen a UFO. Think about that: For every one hundred people, a dozen believe they have seen a UFO.

Have all of these people actually seen a spaceship operated by intelligent beings from some distant place in space? Probably not. To most people, "UFO" means an *extraterrestrial* spacecraft, an airship from another planet. But "UFO" actually stands for "unidentified flying object," which can cover a lot of territory. Some common explanations for UFOs—which turns them into *IFOs,* or *identified* flying objects—are found later in this introduction.

Nevertheless, there are enough sightings that cannot be explained with certainty that the question of whether UFOs exist remains open.

UFOs in the Modern Era

To most people who study UFOs, the "modern era" began in 1947. That year there were many reports of UFOs, and that was when many people began the serious effort to examine UFO reports as scientifically as possible.

Although it was not the first report of the year, the June 24, 1947, sighting by an experienced pilot named Kenneth Arnold was perhaps the most momentous. A respected businessman, Arnold was flying near the Cascade Mountains in Washington state when he saw nine objects speeding, dipping, and gliding through the mountains. Arnold thought they looked like aircraft, but not like any craft he had ever seen. They "were flat as a plate and so smooth that they reflected the sun like a mirror. . . . The things flew like saucers when you make them skip on water,"[3] he reported. Arnold's description inspired a reporter to dub the UFOs "flying saucers," a term that stuck with this type of mysterious sighting for many years.

Arnold's sighting, combined with many others, aroused concern in the U.S. military. World War II had ended only two years before, and one of the U.S. allies in that war—the Soviet Union—was viewed with great suspicion. What if these unidentified aircraft sightings were secret Russian spyplanes or attack planes? Of course, there was the additional possibility that people might actually be seeing extraterrestrial craft. If so, were they a threat to the nation?

The Air Force Gets Involved

By the end of December 1947, the U.S. Air Force had to set up Project Sign at Wright Field (now Wright-Patterson Air Force Base) in Ohio to study all reports of UFOs. One of their first major investigations was of the January 7, 1948, death of Kentucky Air National Guard captain Thomas F. Mantell Jr., who crashed his jet while chasing an elusive UFO. Project Sign determined that Mantell's "UFO" was actually the planet Venus, an explanation few people found believable. (A later investigation suggested that it was a research balloon.)

Project Sign did find some cases that looked like evidence of extraterrestrial visits. But these reports were rejected by the Pentagon, and the project's work decreased in visibility. In late 1948, it was renamed Project Grudge, and investigations started with the premise that UFOs did not exist, that there must be a normal explanation for all UFO reports. Edward J. Ruppelt, Project Grudge's last director, wrote that the group's mission was to "get rid of UFOs."[4] But in September

1951, a wave of UFO sightings and unexplained radar reports near an army radar installation in New Jersey raised air force interest once again.

In March 1952, the investigating group was renamed Project Blue Book, and it remained the air force's UFO investigating arm until 1969. Its first challenge was a major wave of sightings that swept across the nation in 1952, including a radar-confirmed sighting over the White House in July. The two years from October 1951 through September 1953 "emerge as a kind of 'heroic period' of Air Force investigations . . . the one interval during which UFOs were seriously and relatively vigorously investigated,"[5] wrote physicist and UFO investigator James E. McDonald. But after that two-year period, once again the project's mission dwindled. During Project Blue Book's remaining years, its staff was finally reduced to three people, and their objective was to find conventional explanations for the sightings they were able to investigate. They managed to do so for almost all cases. In fact, in the twenty years the air force had an official UFO-investigating group, only about seven hundred of the nearly thirteen thousand cases were declared "unexplained."

Project Blue Book's demise was sealed by the report of the Condon Committee, a University of Colorado group contracted by the government to study all known evidence about UFOs and recommend whether the air force should continue to investigate the puzzling sightings. The Condon Committee was established in part because the public had lost confidence in the air force's honesty about their findings. In 1950, retired Marine Corps major Donald Keyhoe published a widely read article claiming that the air force knew that UFOs were real but were keeping this knowledge from the public. Scientist J. Allen Hynek, who participated in Project Blue Book, told of his discontent with the way the investigations were being handled. Other prominent people also voiced their skepticism about the air force's handling of the UFO investigations.

So Congress decided to have a civilian group of scientists to assess the situation. The University of Colorado agreed to sponsor the investigation, which would be conducted by a committee headed by Edward U. Condon of the university's physics department. Almost from the beginning, the committee's work was controversial. A memo accidentally released to the public suggested to some that the committee had its conclusions planned before it even began work.

Nevertheless, the committee spent two years investigating what was known about UFOs. In January 1969, it presented its fifteen-hundred-page report, which concluded that there was no good reason to continue studying UFOs. There was no evidence to suggest that they existed, said the report, but even if they did, there was no evidence that they threatened the nation; therefore, there was no point for the air force to continue investigating them.

By the end of the year, the air force officially shut down Project Blue Book and its official investigations into UFOs.

Classifying UFOs

J. Allen Hynek was one of the scientists involved in the air force UFO investigations. When he first became involved with Project Blue Book, astrophysicist Hynek was extremely skeptical of UFOs. He believed that the sightings had earthly explanations. But gradually, as he read the reports and talked to witnesses, his opinion changed. Hynek wrote, "In my years of experience in the interrogation of UFO reporters one fact stands out: Invariably I have had the feeling that I was talking to someone who was describing a very *real event.*"[6] He discovered that it was not "nuts" who reported UFOs. Many of the witnesses were scientifically trained, reliable, stable, and well-educated. In many cases, the things they saw could not be explained away.

In his 1972 book *The UFO Experience: A Scientific Inquiry,* Hynek established a classification system for UFOs that is still used by investigators. The system helps organize the many different kinds of UFO experiences. Hynek's categories are:

Nocturnal lights—unexplainable lights in the night sky;

Daylight discs—metallic-looking objects in various forms—round or oval discs, cigar-shapes, triangles, and others;

Radar/visual sightings—visual sightings that are confirmed by unidentifiable radar blips;

Close encounters of the first kind—close sightings—within about two hundred yards—but no interaction with witnesses;

Close encounters of the second kind—the UFO leaves physical traces, such as altered vegetation, indentations in the ground, electromagnetic effects (such as shutting down motors), physical effects on witnesses (such as radiation burns), and others;

Close encounters of the third kind—the witness sees occupants of the UFO.

Since Hynek's death, UFO researchers (called *ufologists*) have added *Close encounters of the fourth kind* to describe reported abductions by UFO occupants (aliens), and some ufologists include *Close encounters of the fifth kind* to designate efforts by humans to contact aliens, often through psychic communication.

This book considers UFOs in the first five categories.

Common Characteristics of UFO Sightings

UFOs come in an amazing variety of shapes and sizes—from gigantic looming airships that resemble the frightening UFO seen in the movie *Independence Day,* to small ships with only enough room for two or three possible occupants, to pure lightforms. UFO shapes have been reported as

saucerlike, bullet-shaped, round, oval, egg-shaped, triangular, boomerang-shaped, rectangular, spherical, hat-shaped—
and some even change shapes before the witnesses' eyes!
Some differences in shape are undoubtedly due to the witness's perspective, time of day or weather conditions, and
objects at the scene (such as trees and buildings) that might
obscure parts of a sky object. If you would like to know
more about the appearance of UFOs, *Spaceships of the Visitors* by Kevin Randle and Russ Estes and *A Fieldguide to UFOs*
by Dennis Stacy and Patrick Huyghe are filled with illustra-
tions showing the many different kinds of UFOs that people
have reported seeing.

Some UFOs have a powerful light effect—a strong light
beam or glow that may be a single color or several colors.
Others are reported to have rows or other arrangements of
lights. Sometimes the lights pulse or move in some kind of
pattern.

Some UFOs are reported to make sounds, while others
are silent. Some move rapidly across the sky, others seem almost playful as they dip and spin, while others hover over a
spot for an extended period of time. Many appear and disappear almost instantaneously.

Many times, witnesses cannot make sense of the UFO's
purpose—it simply appears and then disappears, or it flies
around without any apparent purpose. But some people report that a UFO hovers over a body of water or over a power
facility, leading some ufologists to speculate that the UFO is
acquiring fuel or another necessary commodity.

Some UFOs are reported to leave physical traces—
scorched grass, damaged brush, indentations in the ground,
or elevated radiation levels, for example. Others leave no
measurable evidence behind at all. But they might leave
something not measurable: Some UFOs are said to interfere
with the machinery in the area where they are seen. Many

witnesses report that their car inexplicably stops working just before they see a UFO, then starts up again once the UFO disappears.

UFO witnesses sometimes experience unusual things. Some feel as though they are in a dreamlike state. Some experience "missing time"—that is, they feel like their experience lasted only moments, but when they check the time, they see that it has been hours since the experience began. Some receive a burn or other minor injury during the UFO experience.

Uncommon UFO Connections

Other strange events are sometimes reported in connection with UFOs, but ufologists are not in agreement about what connection, if any, there is between these events and the UFOs. Two common examples are animal mutilations and crop circles.

In the early 1970s, a rash of news stories began reporting strange animal mutilations. Almost without exception, this happened to cattle on western ranches. A cow would be found dead with much of its soft tissue missing—eyes, tongue, ears, udders, and so on. That in itself was not strange—often, if an animal dies, other animals will scavenge parts of the body. But in these cases, the missing organs and tissues appeared to have been carefully excised with surgical skill. Sometimes, before one of these mutilated animals was found, lights would be seen in the sky; sometimes military-style helicopters would be observed. Some people speculated that aliens were killing the cattle for experimental purposes and that the government knew about it and was investigating the scene—that's where the helicopters came in. But another popular theory was that it was the government itself that was doing the cattle killing. The reason involved biological warfare research or some other secret project. Others thought the mutilations were the perfectly natural result of animals and insects.

In the early 1980s in England, some swirled patterns in grain fields began to appear—the first "crop circles." At first these were fairly crude circles and other shapes, but gradually, the designs became more and more elaborate—intertwining circles, braids, depictions of the universe, and so on. These almost exclusively appeared in grain fields, generally appeared overnight, and showed no evidence of a person's trail going into the field to start the pattern. Although two men stepped forward in 1991 and claimed to have hoaxed the crop circles, they remained mysterious. Their patterns were so elaborate that it did not seem possible that they were made by mere humans. *And* witnesses sometimes reported seeing UFOs in an area around the time a crop circle appeared. In the early days, when the crop circles were crude, some people thought they were marks made by a UFO when it landed. As the designs became more sophisticated, some became convinced that they were messages for humanity from the UFO occupants.

Some UFO Explanations and Theories

Misperceptions. If UFOs are not extraterrestrial spacecraft, what are they? Ufologists and others offer many theories. Air force officer John P. Spaulding wrote, "In nineteen years of investigating over 10,000 reports of unidentified flying objects, the evidence has proven almost conclusively that reported aerial phenomena have been either objects created or set aloft by man, generated by atmospheric conditions, or caused by celestial bodies or the residue of meteoric activity."[7]

That covers three explanations—manmade objects (many a UFO has turned into an IFO when it is discovered to have been a misperceived earthly airliner, a piece of satellite debris, or a research balloon); atmospheric conditions (just as a mirage can occur when you are driving down a highway, so one can occur in the sky when conditions are right); and celestial bodies (misidentifications of the planet Venus are a common cause of UFO reports).

It is even possible that a witness has seen an actual UFO-like vehicle unlike any publicly known aircraft. In the 1990s, for example, the Stealth B-2 bomber was a top secret black triangular craft that flew secret experimental flights. It could easily have been mistaken for a triangular UFO.

Psychological explanations. When ordinary causes like these cannot explain a UFO report, investigators turn to other possible explanations. One group of theories involves psychological causes. Many people used think that people who reported seeing a UFO were crazy. However, psychological examinations of UFO experiencers have found that they are as "normal" as people who have not seen UFOs. One study, conducted in 1989 by psychologist Kenneth Ring, found that UFO experiencers were no more likely to be fantasy-prone (subject to having fantasies they believe are real) than anyone else. Ring's results have been confirmed by other studies. Surprisingly, psychiatrist Berthold Schwarz examined thirty-five hundred mental patients and found that *none* of them claimed to have seen a UFO.

Another psychological theory is that people who see UFOs are mentally prepared to see them. UFOs and their alien occupants have become a common part of our popular culture. They are depicted in movies, television programs, computer games, advertisements, and even news publications. We have seen so many fictional depictions of a strange light turning out to be a UFO that when we see an unexplained light or object in the sky our thoughts naturally turn to UFOs.

Some ufologists see "trends" in UFO reports that seem to go along with how they are depicted in news reports and popular culture. For instance, when UFOs were first reported in the 1940s and 1950s, most commonly they were seen as round discs that literally resembled flying saucers. Today, one of the most commonly reported UFO shapes is triangular. Some researchers think that people who report these triangular craft have been influenced by other reports.

Metaphysical explanation. Another theory is that UFOs are real, but they are not nuts-and-bolts vehicles, and their occupants are not flesh-and-blood aliens. Instead, UFOs are metaphysical—they come from another dimension. This dimension may be a future world, or it may be a parallel universe someplace around us. Jacques Vallee, an astrophysicist who has studied UFOs for many years, writes, "I believe the UFO phenomenon *represents evidence for other dimensions beyond spacetime;* the UFOs may not come from ordinary space, but from a *multiverse* which is all around us."[8] His belief comes in part from the impossible things UFOs do—for example, change their shape as a witness watches, and appear or disappear instantaneously. Some people who hold this kind of belief think that the spaceships are watching over Earth, observing and even guiding humanity to its future.

Hoaxes. In addition to these theories and others, a small number of UFO sightings are out-and-out hoaxes. However, UFO reporter Antonio Huneeus says that of the nearly thirteen thousand reports Project Blue Book evaluated, only 116 cases (0.9 percent) were determined to be hoaxes, and of more than two thousand cases investigated by the French space agency, less than 1 percent were hoaxes.[9] False UFOs are much more likely to be caused by misperceptions or delusions than by hoaxes. Nevertheless, we must keep in mind that today's increasingly powerful and inexpensive technology has made it easier than ever to create a convincing fake photograph, videotape, or sound recording.

Secret Evidence

Complicating the UFO question is governmental secrecy. When governments began studying UFOs, the Cold War was on. A time of extreme world tension, the Cold War pitted the United States and the Soviet Union in four decades of competition, threats, and war-brinking activities. Since both superpowers owned thousands of nuclear weapons that could utterly destroy a few square miles or entire nations, their antagonism threatened the safety of the other nations of the world as well. It was entirely possible that UFOs were really spyplanes or nuclear weapons being tested. No one questioned the correctness of governments hiding UFO information when it was a matter of national security. But even when it became clear that UFOs did not represent a security threat, people began to wonder what the government was hiding—and why. Government secrecy was not found in the United States alone. Timothy Good's 1984 book *Above Top Secret: The Worldwide UFO Cover-Up* detailed information formerly hidden by nation after nation.

In the United States, the air force investigated UFOs for twenty years and most of their work was classified "Top Secret" for most of that time. In 1969 the Condon Committee report had admonished that secrecy discouraged confidence in the government and encouraged belief that "a government conspiracy existed to conceal the truth." It added, "Where secrecy is known to exist one can never be absolutely sure that he knows the complete truth."[10]

No truer words could have been written. Because the government was clearly concealing some information and lying—or at least misleading—the public about other information, conspiracy and cover-up theories sprang up and multiplied over the years. Some said that mysterious "Men in Black," who may have been either government agents or aliens, would visit those who had seen UFOs and subtly or boldly threaten them to keep quiet about what they'd seen. Some suggested that the government had actually captured alien craft and occupants and were keeping them at a secret location, usually identified as Wright-Patterson Air Force Base in Ohio or Area 51, a secret military research site in the Nevada desert. Others said that the government was in cahoots with the aliens. One offshoot of this theory was the idea that the government was allowing aliens to do research on humans in exchange for the aliens' advanced technology, which allowed us to develop microchips, laser beams, and other sophisticated tools. Official denial of any of these plots simply fueled the belief of those most suspicious of the government.

In 1966, Congress passed the Freedom of Information Act (FOIA) to make it easier for people to gain access to government records. An individual could request specific information (for example, a certain report), and if it was not classified as secret it would be provided to that individual. In 1974, the act was amended to make it even easier. The requester could provide a general description of the desired information (for example, "any air force records relating to UFOs"), and the government would provide it if it wasn't classified.

Lawrence Fawcett and Barry J. Greenwood, authors of *The UFO Cover-Up: What the Government Won't Say* and members of a group called Citizens Against UFO Secrecy (CAUS), were among the first to attempt to gain all of the government's records on UFOs. The process was not easy, but they and other researchers managed to acquire three thousand previously classified documents by the early 1980s. Many more documents have been obtained since then. Many of the documents were blacked out by censors' pens, but many contained proof that not only the air force had been investigating UFOs; several other U.S. government agencies had been involved as well.

Did the documents definitively prove that UFOs exist? Not really. They *did* prove that what most people suspected was true: The government had been a lot more involved in UFO investigations than it had ever let on, and it had a lot more suggestive information than anyone had suspected. Ufologists tended to think the released documents supported the existence of UFOs, but skeptics (those who don't believe) thought the government's clear failure to discover undeniable evidence was proof that UFOs are a myth. And the government's agonizingly slow release of often-censored documents has done little to restore public confidence that the government is being honest and forthcoming.

In fact, in 1997, the air force released a major report supporting its claim that UFOs and aliens supposedly seen in New Mexico in 1947 were really research balloons and dummies. The Gallup Organization conducted a survey for CNN/*USA Today* that asked whether people believed the report. Sixty-four percent said they did not.[11]

Ongoing Mystery

The UFO mystery is a fascinating one to explore. Although this introduction has focused primarily on UFOs in the United States, UFOs have been seen all over the world by pilots, factory workers, scientists, police officers, farmers, teachers, and others, old and young. Two thousand or more sightings are reported every year—*Life* magazine reported that 2,416 sightings were reported in 1999.[12] And most ufologists believe that many more people see UFOs but don't report them out of fear of being ridiculed. Of the reports that are made, only a small percentage are investigated thoroughly, and many of these are discovered to have some easy explanation. But a small percentage remain unexplained. These are the cases that inspire ufologists to continue their work.

The best available information tends to be about older

cases, several of which have been thoroughly investigated. But UFOs are still being reported, worldwide, nearly daily. Some of these reports can be found on websites such as The Center for Physical Trace Research (www.angelfire.com), *U* UFO Database (www.larryhatch.com), and the National UFO Reporting Center (www.msatech.com). These sites accept reports from anyone who has seen a UFO. But if you look at these reports, keep in mind that they have *not* been investigated. As with Project Blue Book, probably 95 percent of these can be explained by various mundane reasons—weather or astronomical phenomena, optical illusions, and even hoaxes. It is that small percentage of cases that are not easily explained that keep investigators busy looking for answers.

This book is divided into four sections that aim to help you evaluate the UFO information that comes your way.

Notes

1. Quoted in Don Berliner et al., *UFO Briefing Document: The Best Available Evidence*, New York: Dell, 2000, p.186.

2. Frank Newport and Maura Strausberg, "Americans' Belief in Psychic and Paranormal Phenomena Is Up over Last Decade," June 8, 2001, www.gallup.com.

3. Quoted in Michael Hesemann, *UFOs: The Secret History*. New York: Marlowe & Company, 1998, p. 31.

4. Quoted in Jerome Clark, *The UFO Book: Encyclopedia of the Extraterrestrial*. Detroit: Visible Ink Press, a div. of Gale Research, 1998, p. 487.

5. Ibid., p. 466.

6. J. Allen Hynek, *The UFO Experience: A Scientific Inquiry*. Chicago: Henry Regnery, 1972, p. 12.

7. Quoted in John Robert Colombo, *The UFO Quote Book*. Toronto: Colombo Publishing, 1999, p. 292.

8. Jacques Vallee, *Dimensions: A Casebook of Alien Contact*. New York: Ballantine, 1988, p. 253.

9. Antonio Huneeus, "UFO Hoaxes," *FATE*, September 1994, p. 36.

10. Edward U. Condon et al., *Final Report of the Scientific Study of Unidentified Flying Objects*. New York: E.P. Dutton, 1969, pp. 520, 522.

11. ". . . The Public Makes Smart Distinctions," *The Public Perspective*, December/January 1998, p. 11.

12. Cynthia Fox, "The Search for Extraterrestrial Life: Why on Earth Do We Still Believe?" *Life*, March 1, 2000, p. 46.

Chapter 1

UFOs Are Fact

Flying Saucers Are Real

Kenneth J. Arnold

On June 24, 1947, thirty-two-year-old Kenneth J. Arnold, pilot and businessman, saw something he would never forget. While on a flight over the Cascade Mountains between Chehalis to Yakima, Washington, he saw nine flying objects that didn't resemble any aircraft he knew, and Arnold was very familiar with the aircraft that flew the 1947 skies. But these objects were different. He wondered if they could be experimental aircraft, but none of the objects had a tail as he would have expected any aircraft to have.

The next day he told newspaper reporters at an airshow in Pendleton, Oregon, that the objects had flown incredibly fast and moved "like speedboats on rough water," or "like a saucer would if you skipped it across the water." The latter phrase led reporter William C. Burquette to coin the term "flying saucer," which stuck as the most popular description of unidentified flying objects for years to come. The Pendleton newspaper's brief account of Arnold's sighting was

Excerpted from Kenneth J. Arnold's Report to the Commanding General at Wright Patterson Air Force Base, July 12, 1947.

23

picked up by the national press, and Arnold and flying saucers became famous.

Nearly three weeks after his experience, Arnold was interviewed by FBI Officer-in-Charge Frank M. Brown. Brown stated in his report on July 16 that "It is the personal opinion of the interviewer that [Arnold] actually saw what he states he saw in the attached report." In addition to being impressed by Arnold's good character and his knowledge about aircraft, Brown believed that Arnold would not have been likely to make up such a story because it would undoubtedly subject him to ridicule.

The following article is excerpted from Arnold's account as he wrote it for military officials on July 12.

M y flying experience started as a boy in Minot, North Dakota, where I took my first flying lesson from Earl T. Vance, who was originally from Great Falls, Montana. Due to the high cost at that time, I was unable to continue my flying and did not fly of any great consequence until 1943. I was given my pilot certificate by Ed Leach, a senior CAA [Civil Aviation Authority] inspector of Portland, Oregon, and for the last three years have owned my own airplane, covering my entire territory with same and flying from forty to one hundred hours per month since. Due to the fact that I use an airplane entirely in my work, in January of this year I purchased a new Callair airplane, which is an airplane designed for high altitude take-offs and short rough field use.

In the type of flying I do, it takes a great deal of practice and judgment to be able to land in most any cow pasture and get out without injuring your airplane; the runways are very limited and the altitude is very high in some of the fields and places I have to go in my work. To date, I have landed in 823 cow pastures in mountain meadows, and in over a thousand hours a flat tire has been my greatest mishap.

The Sighting

The following story of what I observed over the Cascade mountains, as impossible as it may seem, is positively true. I never asked nor wanted any notoriety for just accidentally being in the right spot at the right time to observe what I did. I reported something that I know any pilot would have reported. I don't think that in any way my observation was due to any sensitivity of eye sight or judgment than what is considered normal for any pilot.

On 24 June, Tuesday, 1947, I had finished my work for the Central Air Service at Chehalis, Washington, and at about two o'clock I took off from Chehalis, Washington, airport with the intention of going to Yakima, Wash. My trip was delayed for an hour to search for a large marine transport that supposedly went down near or around the southwest side of Mt. Rainier in the State of Washington and to date has never been found

I flew directly toward Mt. Rainier after reaching an altitude of about 9,500 feet, which is the approximate elevation of the high plateau from which Mt. Rainier rises. I had made one sweep of this high plateau to the westward, searching all of the various ridges for this marine ship and flew to the west down and near the ridge side of the canyon where Ashford, Washington, is located.

Unable to see anything that looked like the lost ship, I made a 300 degree turn to the right and above the little city of Mineral, starting again toward Mt. Rainier. I climbed back up to an altitude of approximately 9,200 feet.

The air was so smooth that day that it was a real pleasure flying and, as most pilots do when the air is smooth and they are flying at a higher altitude, I trimmed out my airplane in the direction of Yakima, Washington, which was almost directly east of my position, and simply sat in my plane observing the sky and the terrain.

There was a DC-4 to the left and to the rear of me approximately fifteen miles distance, and I should judge, at 14,000 foot elevation.

A Bright Flash

The sky and air was as clear as crystal. I hadn't flown more than two or three minutes on my course when a bright flash reflected on my airplane. It startled me as I thought I was too close to some other aircraft. I looked every place in the sky and couldn't find where the reflection had come from until I looked to the left and the north of Mt. Rainier where I observed a chain of nine peculiar looking aircraft flying from north to south at approximately 9,500 foot elevation and going, seemingly, in a definite direction of about 170 degrees.

They were approaching Mt. Rainier very rapidly, and I merely assumed they were jet planes. Anyhow, I discovered that this was where the reflection had come from, as two or three of them every few seconds would dip or change their course slightly, just enough for the sun to strike them at an angle that reflected brightly on my plane.

These objects being quite far away, I was unable for a few seconds to make out their shape or their formation. Very shortly they approached Mt. Rainier, and I observed their outline against the snow quite plainly.

I thought it was very peculiar that I couldn't find their tails but assumed they were some type of jet planes. I was determined to clock their speed, as I had two definite points I could clock them by; the air was so clear that it was very easy to see objects and determine their approximate shape and size at almost fifty miles that day.

I remember distinctly that my sweep second hand on my

eight day clock, which is located on my instrument panel, read one minute to 3 P.M. as the first object of this formation passed the southern edge of Mt. Rainier. I watched these objects with great interest as I had never before observed airplanes flying so close to the mountain tops, flying directly south to the southeast down the hog's back of a mountain range. I would estimate their elevation could have varied a thousand feet one way or another up or down, but they were pretty much on the horizon to me which would indicate they were near the same elevation as I was.

They flew like many times I have observed geese to fly in a rather diagonal chain-like line as if they were linked together. They seemed to hold a definite direction but rather swerved in and out of the high mountain peaks. Their speed at the time did not impress me particularly, because I knew that our army and air forces had planes that went very fast.

Saucerlike Objects

What kept bothering me as I watched them flip and flash in the sun right along their path was the fact I couldn't make out any tail on them, and I am sure that any pilot would justify more than a second look at such a plane.

I observed them quite plainly, and I estimate my distance from them, which was almost at right angles, to be between twenty to twenty-five miles. I knew they must be very large to observe their shape at that distance, even on as clear a day as it was that Tuesday.

In fact I compared a zeus fastener or cowling tool I had in my pocket with them, holding it up on them and holding it up on the DC-4 that I could observe at quite a distance to my left, and they seemed smaller than the DC-4; but, I should judge their span would have been as wide as the furtherest engines on each side of the fuselage of the DC-4.

The more I observed these objects, the more upset I became, as I am accustomed and familiar with most all objects flying whether I am close to the ground or at higher altitudes. I observed the chain of these objects passing another high snow-covered ridge in between Mt. Rainier and Mt. Adams, and as the first one was passing the south crest of this ridge the last object was entering the northern crest of the ridge. As I was flying in the direction of this particular ridge, I measured it and found it to be approximately five miles so I could safely assume that the chain of these saucer-like objects at least five miles long. I could quite accurately determine their pathway due to the fact that there were several high peaks that were a little this side of them as well as higher peaks on the other side of their pathway.

As the last unit of this formation passed the southern most high snow-covered crest of Mt. Adams, I looked at my sweep second hand and it showed that they had travelled the distance in one minute and forty-two seconds. Even at the time this timing did not upset me as I felt confident after I would land there would be some explanation of what I saw.

A number of news men and experts suggested that I might have been seeing reflections or even a mirage. This I know to be absolutely false, as I observed these objects not only through the glass of my airplane but turned my airplane sideways where I could open my window and observe them with a completely unobstructed view. (Without sun glasses)

Even though two minutes seems like a very short time to one on the ground, in the air in two minutes time a pilot can observe a great many things and anything within his sight of vision probably as many as fifty or sixty times.

I continued my search for the marine plane for another fifteen or twenty minutes and while searching for this marine plane, what I had just observed kept going through my mind. I became more disturbed, so after taking a last look at Tieton Reservoir I headed for Yakima.

Some Type of Aircraft?

I might add that my complete observation of these objects, which I could even follow by flashes as they passed Mt. Adams, was around two and one-half or three minutes, although, by the time they reached Mt. Adams, they were out of my range of vision as far as determining shape or form. Of course, when the sun reflected from one or two or three of those units, they appeared to be completely round; but, I am making a drawing to the best of my ability, which I am including, as to the shape I observed these objects to be as they passed the snow covered ridges as well as Mt. Rainier. When these objects were flying approximately straight and level, they were just a black thin line and when they flipped was the only time I could get a judgment as to their size.

These objects were holding an almost constant elevation; they did not seem to be going up or to be coming down, such as would be the case of rockets or artillery shells. I am convinced in my own mind that they were some type of airplane, even though they didn't conform with the many aspects of the conventional type of planes that I know.

A UFO Crashed Near Roswell, New Mexico

Charles Berlitz and William L. Moore

In 1980, a slim little book called *The Roswell Incident* claimed to tell the story of "the most important UFO encounter in our century." It reported on an incident that had supposedly occurred in July 1947 near Roswell, New Mexico. The authors interviewed witnesses who said that more than thirty years before, they had seen a crashed alien spacecraft, found debris "not of this earth," and even seen the bodies of small, alien beings being carted away by U.S. military authorities, never to be seen again. The book caused something of a sensation, but was only the first in a continuing series of books devoted to investigation of and debate about the Roswell incident.

There's no question that something happened near Roswell at that time, but the question of what it was is still argued today. It's a fact that something crashed and that debris was found. It's a fact that the local air base issued a statement saying that it had "captured" a flying saucer. But it's also a fact that an air force brigadier general issued a statement later that same day saying that the first statement was in error, that what had actually been found was a weather balloon that had crashed while conducting research. Beyond these basic facts, just about everything about the Roswell incident is open to question. If a UFO did crash, all traces of it were removed or have been lost over time. So investigators are left to rely on often-conflicting expert testimony and eyewitness accounts of something that happened three decades or more in the past. Since it first recanted the flying saucer report, the air force has held to its claim that it was a balloon that crashed. But other experts insist that the air force's argument does not hold up under close scrutiny.

The Roswell Incident included the testimony of several eyewitnesses, including that of Jesse A. Marcel, who was a major at Roswell Army Air Field in 1947. William L. Moore and another researcher, Stanton Friedman, interviewed him several times in 1979. The article below is taken from those interviews. Marcel also talks about Mac Brazel, on whose land the debris was found.

Charles Berlitz has written several popular books on paranormal topics, including the *Bermuda Triangle* and *Atlantis*. William L. Moore is a UFO investigator.

QUESTION: *Major Marcel, did you personally see a crashed UFO?*

I saw a lot of wreckage but no complete machine. Whatever it was had to have exploded in the air above ground level. It had disintegrated before it hit the ground. The wreckage was scattered over an area of about three quarters of a mile long and several hundred feet wide.

How did the Roswell Base know about the crash at Brazel's ranch?

We heard about it on July 7 when we got a call from the county sheriff's office at Roswell. I was eating lunch at the officers' club when the call came through saying that I should go out and talk to Brazel. The sheriff said that Brazel had told him that something had exploded over Brazel's ranch and that there was a lot of debris scattered around.

I finished my lunch and went into town to talk to this fellow. When I had heard what he had to say, I decided that this was a matter that had better be brought to the attention of the colonel [Colonel Blanchard] right away and let him decide what ought to be done. I wanted Brazel to accompany me back to the base with his truck, but he said he had some things to do first and could he meet me somewhere in an hour or so. I arranged for him to meet me at the sheriff's office, and went back to see the colonel.

In my discussion with the colonel, we determined that a downed aircraft of some unusual sort might be involved, so the colonel said I had better get out there, and to take whatever I needed and go. I and a CIC [Counter-Intelligence Corps] agent from West Texas by the name of Cavitt [Marcel couldn't recall his first name] followed this man out to his ranch, with me driving my staff car [a '42 Buick] and Cavitt in a Jeep Carry-all. There were almost no roads, and at spots we literally had to go right across country. It was as close to the middle of nowhere as you could get. Anyhow, we got there very late in the afternoon and had to spend the night with this fellow. All we had to eat was some cold pork and beans and some crackers.

Brazel's Account

Brazel lived on the southeast side of Corona—quite far. The closest town was thirty miles away. He lived in a dinky house on a sheep ranch—no radio, no telephone—lived there by himself most of the time. His wife and kids lived in Tularosa or Carrizozo [Note: It was Tularosa.] so the children would have some place to attend school.

It seems to me that Brazel told me that he thought he had heard an odd explosion late in the evening several days earlier during an electrical storm, but paid no special attention to it at the time because he had attributed it to just a freak part of the storm. He didn't find the wreckage until the next morning.

On Saturday, July 5, 1947, Brazel went into town— Corona. While he was there he heard stories about flying saucers having been seen all over the area. He began to think that's what had come down on his ranch, but I don't know whether he said anything about it to anyone at the time.

On Sunday, July 6, Brazel decided he had better go into town and report this to someone. When he got there, he went to the Chaves County sheriff's office and told the story to the sheriff. It was the sheriff, George Wilcox, who called me at the base. I was eating lunch at the time and had just sat down when the phone rang.

Not a Weather Balloon

Do you think that what you saw was a weather balloon?

It was not. I was pretty well acquainted with most everything that was in the air at that time, both ours and foreign. I was also acquainted with virtually every type of weather-observation or radar tracking device being used by either the civilians or the military. It was definitely not a weather or tracking device, nor was it any sort of plane or missile. What it was we didn't know. We just picked up the fragments. It was something I had never seen before, or since, for that matter. I didn't know what it was, but it certainly wasn't anything built by us and it most certainly wasn't any weather balloon.

Can you describe the materials that you found on the site?

There was all kinds of stuff—small beams about three eighths or a half inch square with some sort of hieroglyphics on them that nobody could decipher. These looked something like balsa wood, and were of about the same weight, except that they were not wood at all. They were very hard, although flexible, and would not burn. There was a great deal of an unusual parchment-like substance which was brown in color and extremely strong, and a great number of small pieces of a metal like tinfoil, except that it wasn't tinfoil. I was interested in electronics and kept looking for something that resembled instruments or electronic equipment, but I didn't find anything. One of the other fellows, Cavitt, I think, found a black, metallic-looking box several inches square. As there was no apparent way to open this, and since it didn't appear to be an instrument package of any sort (it too was very lightweight), we threw it in with the rest of the stuff. I don't know what eventually happened to the box, but it went along with the rest of the material we eventually took to Fort Worth.

What was especially interesting about the material?

One thing that impressed me about the debris was the fact that a lot of it looked like parchment. It had little numbers with symbols that we had to call hieroglyphics because I could not understand them. They could not be read, they were just like symbols, something that meant something, and they were not all the same, but the same general pattern, I would say. They were pink and purple. They looked like they were painted on. These little numbers could not be broken, could not be burned. I even took my cigarette lighter and tried to burn the material we found that resembled parchment and balsa, but it would not burn—wouldn't even smoke. But something that is even more astounding is that the pieces of metal that we brought back were so thin, just like the tinfoil in a pack of cigarettes. I didn't pay too much attention to that at first, until one of the boys came to me and said: "You know that metal that was in there? I tried to bend the stuff and it won't bend. I even tried it with a sledgehammer. You can't make a dent on it." . . . This particular piece of metal was about two feet long and maybe a foot wide. It was so light it weighed practically nothing, that was true of all the material that was brought up, it weighed practically nothing . . . it was so thin. So I tried to bend the stuff. We did all we could to bend it. It would not bend and you could not tear it or cut it either. We even tried making a dent in it with a sixteen-pound sledgehammer, and there was still no dent in it. . . . It's still a mystery to me what the whole thing was. Now by bend, I mean crease. It was possible to flex this stuff back and forth, even to wrinkle it, but you could not put a crease in it that would stay, nor could you dent it at all. I would almost have to describe it as a metal with plastic properties. One of the fellows tried to put some of the pieces together—like a jigsaw puzzle. He managed to get about ten square feet together, but it wasn't enough to get any idea of the general shape of the object itself. Whatever it was, it was big.

Dealing with the Debris

What did you do with the material you had picked up?

We collected all the debris we could handle. When we had filled the Carry-all, I began to fill the trunk and back seat of the Buick. That afternoon [July 7] we headed back to Roswell and arrived there in the early evening.

When we arrived there, we discovered that the story that we had found a flying disc had leaked out ahead of us. We had an eager-beaver PIO [public information officer] on the base who had taken it upon himself to call the AP [Associated Press] on this thing. We had several calls that night, and one reporter even came to the house, but of course I couldn't confirm anything to them over the phone, and the man who came to the house my wife sent over to see the colonel. The next morning that written press release went out, and after that things really hit the fan. The phone rang right off the hook. I heard that the brass fried him later on for putting out that press release, but then I can't say so for sure. . . .

Anyway, that next afternoon we loaded everything into a B-29 on orders from Colonel Blanchard and flew it all to Fort Worth. I was scheduled to fly it all the way to Wright Field in Ohio, but when we got to Carswell at Fort Worth, the general nixed it. He took control at this point, told the press it was all a weather balloon, and ordered me not to talk to the press under any circumstances. I was pulled off the flight and someone else was assigned to fly the stuff up to Wright [Patterson] Field. Everything was sent to Wright-Patterson for analysis.

Just after we got to Carswell, Fort Worth, we were told to bring some of this stuff up to the general's office—that he wanted to take a look at it. We did this and spread it out on the floor on some brown paper.

What we had was only a very small portion of the debris—there was a whole lot more. There was half a B-29-ful outside. General Ramey allowed some members of the press in to take a picture of this stuff. They took one picture of me on the floor holding up some of the less-interesting metallic debris. The press was allowed to photograph this, but were not allowed far enough into the room to touch it. The stuff in that one photo was pieces of the actual stuff we had found. It was not a staged photo. Later, they cleared out our wreckage and substituted some of their own. Then they allowed more photos. Those photos were taken while the actual wreckage was already on its way to Wright Field. I was not in these. I believe these were taken with the general and one of his aides. I've seen a lot of weather balloons, but I've never seen one like that before. And I don't think they ever did either.

Let's go back to how the press and radio people got involved. Can we go over that again?

It was the public information officer, Haut I believe his name was, who called the AP and later wrote the press release. I heard he wasn't authorized to do this, and I believe he was severely reprimanded for it, I think all the way from Washington. We had calls from everywhere—all over the world. It was General Ramey who put up the cover story about the balloon just to get the press off our backs. The press was told it was just a balloon and that the flight to Wright-Patterson was canceled; but all that really happened was that I was removed from the flight and someone else took it up to W-P. I wasn't even allowed to talk to the press except to say what the general had told me to say. They all wanted to ask me questions, and I couldn't tell them anything.

A Cover-Up

So what you're saying is that this whole weather-balloon thing was nothing but a cover-up?

Well, one thing that I want to point out is that the newsmen saw very little of the material—and none of the important things that had hieroglyphics, or markings, on them. They didn't see that because it wasn't there. They wanted me to tell them about it but I couldn't say anything. When the general came in he told me not to say anything, that he would handle it. He told the newsmen: "Yes, that's the weather balloon." So the newsmen had to take his word for it because they had nothing else to go by. They tried to get me to talk about it, but the general had told me not to say anything and I couldn't say anything. That's when the general told me: "It's best you go back to Roswell. You have duties to perform there. We'll handle it from here."

Evidence: Physical Traces in France

Don Berliner with Marie Galbraith and
Antonio Huneeus

Most UFOs have only eyewitnesses to confirm their existence. But scientists often aren't convinced by eyewitnesses alone. So when a rare case comes along in which physical traces are left by a UFO, UFO investigators are ecstatic. An incident near Trans-en-Provence, France, on January 8, 1981, was such a case. Although there was only one eyewitness, the French UFO investigations organization, GEPAN, was on the scene the day after the occurrence. Investigators interviewed the witness, examined the UFO landing site, and took soil samples to be analyzed for irregularities. The tests showed that, indeed, the plants in the area had been changed by whatever had happened on January 8.

Some people call this case the best-investigated of all time. Many consider it to be the most convincing as well.

The following is taken from a special report funded by wealthy American philanthropist Laurence Rockefeller, who wanted to collect the best available evidence about UFOs to encourage further study of the phenomenon. His associate Marie Galbraith supervised the project, and internationally known UFO investigators Don Berliner and Antonio Huneeus assembled the cases. Initially, only about one thousand copies of the report were published, and they were sent to select politicians, world leaders, and scientists in 1996. In 2000, it was published in paperback form so the information would be accessible to the general public.

O n the afternoon of January 8, 1981, a strange craft landed on a farm near the village of Trans-en-Provence in the Var region in southeastern France. Physical traces left on the ground were collected by the gendarmerie within twenty-four hours and later analyzed in several French government laboratories. Extensive evidence of anomalous activity was detected.

The case was investigated by the Groupe d'Études des Phénomènes Aérospatiaux Non-identifiés (GEPAN), or Unidentified Aerospace Phenomena Study Group, established in 1977 within the National Center for Space Studies (CNES) in Toulouse, the French counterpart of NASA. (The functions of GEPAN were reorganized in 1988 into the Service d'Expertise des Phénomènes de Rentrées Atmosphériques, or SEPRA.) The primary investigator was Jean-Jacques Velasco, the head of SEPRA.

The witness was the farmer Renato Nicolai, age 55, on whose property the UFO landed and then took off almost immediately. Thinking that it was a military experimental device, Nicolai notified the local gendarmes on the following day. The gendarmes interviewed Nicolai and collected soil and plant samples from the landing site within twenty-four hours of the occurrence, notifying GEPAN on January

12 as part of a cooperation agreement for UFO investigation between the two agencies. Further collection of samples and measurements of the site were undertaken by the GEPAN team, and the samples were thoroughly analyzed by several government laboratories.

Eyewitness Report

The first detailed report on the case was published by GEPAN in 1983. Nicolai's testimony to the police was simple and straightforward:

My attention was drawn to a small noise, a kind of little whistling. I turned around and I saw, in the air, a ship which was just about the height of a pine tree at the edge of my property. This ship was not turning but was descending toward the ground. I only heard a slight whistling. I saw no flames, neither underneath or around the ship.

While the ship was continuing to descend, I went closer to it, heading toward a little cabin. I was able to see very well above the roof. From there I saw the ship standing on the ground.

At that moment, the ship began to emit another whistling, a constant, consistent whistling. Then it took off and once it was at the height of the trees, it took off rapidly . . . toward the northeast. As the ship began to lift off, I saw beneath it four openings from which neither smoke nor flames were emitting. The ship picked up a little dust when it left the ground.

I was at that time about 30 meters [100 feet] from the landing site. I thereafter walked towards the spot and I noticed a circle about two meters [7 feet] in diameter. At certain spots on the curve of the circle, there were tracks (or traces).

The ship was in the form of two saucers upside down, one against the other. It must have been about 1.5 meters [5 feet] high. It was the color of lead. The ship had a border or type of brace around its circumference. Underneath the brace, as it took off, I saw two kinds of round pieces which could have been landing gear or feet. There were also two circles which looked like trap doors. The two feet, or landing gear, extended about 20 centimeters [8 inches] beneath the body of the whole ship.

Soil and Plant Analysis

The samples of soil and wild alfalfa collected from the landing site, as well as the control samples from varying distances from the epicenter, were subjected to a number of analyses: physico-chemical analysis at the SNEAP laboratory [a French scientific laboratory], electronic diffraction studies at Toulouse University, mass spectrometry by ion bombardment at the University of Metz, and biochemical analysis of the vegetable samples at the National Institute of Agronomy Research (INRA), among others.

The Trans-en-Provence case is very likely the most thoroughly scientifically documented CE-II (Close Encounter of the Second Kind) ever investigated. Some of the scientific findings included:

Traces were still perceptible 40 days after the event.

There was a strong mechanical pressure forced (probably the result of a heavy weight) on the surface.

A thermatic heating of the soil, perhaps consecutive to or immediately following the shock, the value of which did not exceed 600 degrees.

The chlorophyll pigment in the leaf samples was weakened from 30 to 50 percent . . . The young leaves withstood the most serious losses, evolving toward the content and composition more characteristic of old leaves.

The action of nuclear irradiation does not seem to be analogous with the energy source implied with the observed phenomenon; on the other hand, a specific intensification of the transformation of chlorophyll . . . could be tied to the action of a type of electric energy field.

On the biochemical level, the analysis was made on the entirety of the factors of photosynthesis, lipids, sugars and amino acids. There were many differences between those samples further from the spot of the landing and those that were closer to the spot.

It was possible to qualitatively show the occurrence of an important event which brought with it deformations of the terrain caused by mass, mechanics, a heating effect, and perhaps certain transformations and deposits of trace minerals. We cannot give a precise and unique interpretation to this remarkable combination of results. We can state that there is, nonetheless, another confirmation of a very significant event which happened on this spot.

Most of the puzzling biochemical mutations were discovered by Michel Bounias of INRA. Describing the young leaves to a journalist from *France-Soir* magazine, Bounias stated in 1983:

From an anatomical and physiological point, they [leaves] had all the characteristics of their age, but they presented the biochemical characteristics of leaves of an advanced age: old leaves! And that doesn't resemble anything that we know on our planet.

In a technical report published in the *Journal of Scientific Exploration*, Bounias concluded:

It was not the aim of the author to identify the exact nature of the phenomenon observed on the 8th of January 1981 at Trans-en-Provence. But it can reasonably be concluded that something unusual did occur that might be consistent, for instance, with an electromagnetic source of stress. The most striking coincidence is that at the same time, French physicist J.P. Petit was plotting the equations that led, a few years later, to the evidence that flying objects could be propelled at very high speeds without turbulence nor shock waves using the magnetohydrodynamic effects of Laplace force action!

Other Cases with Physical Traces

Out of a total of twenty-five hundred reports collected officially in France since 1977 and investigated by GEPAN, this case and three other ground-trace incidents (where strange

Cases with Physiological Signs

ENQUIRY CASE	VISIBLE SIGNS (PLANTS)	TYPE OF ANALYSIS	LABORATORY	SUGGESTED INTERPRETATION	STUDY
CHRISTELLE 27/11/79	Grass flattened in given direction	Plant physiology	UPS Toulouse Pr. TOUZE	None	Mechanical properties of grass tissue
TRANS-EN-PROVENCE 08/01/81	Alfalfa leaves withered	Biochemical	INRA Avignon Pr. BOUNIAS	Electromagnetic field Microwaves	Effect of microwaves on plants
AMARANTE 21/08/82	Grass raised Amaranth leaves withered, fruits burst	Plant physiology	UPS Toulouse Pr. ABRAVANEL	Electromagnetic field Microwaves	Effect of lightning on plants
JOE LE TAXI 07/09/87	Birch leaves damaged	Biochemical	INRA Pr. BOUNIAS	Electromagnetic field Microwaves	Effect of microwaves on plants

Chart of four UFO cases with physiological signs on vegetation. Courtesy of CNES/SEPRA.

ground traces were left after alleged UFO landings) continue to puzzle the original investigator, Jean-Jacques Velasco. At a meeting of the Society for Scientific Exploration (SSE) in Glasgow in 1994, Velasco summarized the "four noteworthy cases" with "effects observed on vegetation":

These cases have all been the subject of enquiries by the police, then GEPAN or SEPRA. In each of these situations, a UAP [Unidentified Aerospace Phenomena] was observed in direct relation in a zone perturbed by the phenomenon.

1. "Christelle" case of 27/11/1979: Persistence of flattened grass several days after the observation. The samples taken and analyzed by a plant biology laboratory at Toulouse University did not give unequivocal evidence of chemical or biological disturbance of the samples taken from the marked area relative to controls. A study of the mechanical properties of grass tissue subjected to strong mechanical pressure showed that the duration is a more important factor than the mass.

2. "Trans-en-Provence" case of 8/01/81: Apparition of a circular print in a crown shape after observation of a metallic object resting on the ground. The vegetation, a kind of wild alfalfa, showed withering of the dried leaves in the central part of the print. The analyses revealed damage of a specific kind affecting the functional relationships of the photosynthetic system.

3. "Amarante" case of 21/08/82: Severe drying of the stems and leaves on a bush (amaranth), punctuated by the appearance of raised blades of grass before the phenomenon disappeared. Biochemical analyses revealed that no reported outside agent could be the cause of such effects. Only a corona effect due to powerful electromagnetic fields could partially explain the observations.

4. "Joe Le Taxi" case of 7/09/87: Leaf damage on a tree (birch) and functional disturbance of the photosynthetic system after an intense light and sound phenomenon had been observed. This case demonstrated the importance of good sample collection and preservation for biochemical analysis.

Of these four cases, Trans-en-Provence still remains the

best documented. Velasco concluded that, after years of investigations:

> The laboratory conclusion that seems to best cover the effects observed and analyzed is that of a powerful emission of electromagnetic fields, pulsed or not, in the microwave frequency range.

SEPRA's latest thrust in the investigation has centered on "experimentally reproducing in the laboratory continuous and pulsed emissions of microwave fields at various powers and frequencies so as to verify biochemical effects on plants." While the studies are still preliminary, Velasco concluded his SSE presentation with the following statement:

> However these initial studies carried out to validate the hypothesis of microwave action on the biological activity of plants in relation with UAPs need to be extended if we are to understand the mechanisms involved at molecular scale. Similarly, an investigation of the frequency range, the power and the exposure time would be useful to confirm the hypothesis of microwaves combined with other fields of electromagnetic forces coming into play in the propulsion of UAPs.

Evidence: Radar and Visual Sighting in Tehran

Lawrence Fawcett and Barry J. Greenwood

In Tehran, Iran, on September 19, 1976, a mysterious incident occurred that many people believe is convincing evidence for the existence of UFOs. On that night, military F-14 jet planes engaged a UFO. The incident had several convincing elements: There were many witnesses, both civilian and military, and several were experienced pilots. The UFO was seen on radar. The UFO apparently affected the jets' electrical and communication systems, suggesting both a superior technology and an intelligence that controlled it.

The following article describes the incident and includes excerpts from official documents. The authors, Lawrence Fawcett and Barry J. Greenwood, have been involved in UFO investigations for many years. At the time they wrote this account, both men were active in CAUS (Citizens Against UFO Secrecy), an organization devoted to pressuring the U.S. government to stop hiding past and present information about UFOs.

In Iran, just one month after a UFO sighting in Tunisia, one of the most sensational UFO incidents in recent years took place. The first public indications that something extraordinary happened on September 19, 1976, appeared in the English language *Kayhan International*, published in Tehran, Iran. It stated in the September 25 edition:

> And now . . . the REAL story about that "UFO." Unfortunately, it's not quite as exciting as the tales we've been hearing over the last day or two about the bright light "thing" that allegedly had the audacity to chase two jets of the Imperial Iranian Air Force across Tehran.
>
> Nevertheless, the true facts as outlined by an official source this week still have the ring of science fiction about them.
>
> The source said individuals telephoned Mehrabad Airport's control tower to report a bright light in the night sky. Two jets were scrambled to investigate and one of the pilots reported seeing an object with a light so bright it illuminated the ground below. But the apparition soon disappeared and . . . that's it.
>
> The pilot did not report seeing red, blue, and green flashing lights as the newspaper reports said. And, most emphatically, said the source, it did not switch round and chase the jets.
>
> The newspaper reports also said that when the object came to within five kilometers of the jets, all electrical appliances on the aircraft went out of action, they lost radio contact with the ground and could not fire on the objects as they intended.
>
> "Not so," said the official. "The pilots made no attempt to open fire, and at no time did the aircrafts' electronic gear fail to function."
>
> And, since everything on the plane from controls to fuel pump is electronically operated, it's a little puzzling to figure

out how the plane could possibly have kept in the air anyway.

The official summed it all up by saying the reports, which first appeared in afternoon papers this week, were "exaggerated." A reported verbatim conversation between Pilot "J" and ground control, in which he reported the different lights and the chase, left the official "frankly puzzled."

But he agreed that there was no apparent explanation for what the pilot DID see.

Judging from the newspaper report, the sighting amounted to nothing more than a light in the sky. Rumors of jet chases and electrical failures were "exaggerated," according to officials. But the rumors originated from the Iranian Air Force! What were the facts behind this confusion?

A Military Report

As a result of this kind of publicity, UFO researchers sprang into action. One individual, Charles Huffer, a teacher at the Berlin American High School in Germany, attempted to locate information from the files of the Secretary of Defense relating to the Iranian report. They denied this request in a July 5, 1977, letter. Huffer appealed the decision and finally obtained the release of a three-page message about the report on August 31, 1977, via the Defense Intelligence Agency (DIA). The details are fascinating.

> This report forwards information concerning the sighting of a UFO in Iran on 19 September 1976.
>
> A. At about 1230 A.M. on 19 Sep. 76 the (deleted) received four telephone calls from citizens living in the Shemiran area of Tehran saying that they had seen strange objects in the sky. Some reported a kind of bird-like object while others reported a helicopter with a light on. There were no helicopters airborne at that time.
>
> After he told the citizens it was only stars and had talked to Mehrabad Tower, he decided to look for himself. He noticed an object in the sky similar to a star bigger and

brighter. He decided to scramble an F-4 from Shahrokhi AFB to investigate.

B. At 0130 hrs on the 19th the F-4 took off and proceeded to a point about 40 NM north of Tehran. Due to its brilliance, the object was easily visible from 70 miles away. As the F-4 approached a range of 25 NM, he lost all instrumentation and communications (UHF and intercom). He broke off the intercept and headed back to Shahrokhi. When the F-4 turned away from the object and apparently was no longer a threat to it, the aircraft regained all instrumentation and communications. At 0140 hrs a second F-4 was launched. The backseater acquired a radar lock on at 27 NM 12 o'clock high position with the VC (rate of closure) at 150 NMPH. As the range decreased to 25 NM the object moved away at a speed that was visible on the radar scope and stayed at 25 NM.

C. The size of the radar return was comparable to that of a 707 tanker. The visual size of the object was difficult to discern because of its intense brilliance. The light that it gave off was that of flashing strobe lights arranged in a rectangular pattern and alternating blue, green, red, and orange in color. The sequence of the lights was so fast that all the colors could be seen at once. The object and the pursuing F-4 continued on a course to the south of Tehran when another brightly lighted object, estimated to be one-half to one-third the apparent size of the moon, came out of the original object. This second object headed straight toward the F-4 at a very fast rate of speed. The pilot attempted to fire an AIM-9 missile at the object but at that instant his weapons control panel went off and he lost all communications (UHF and interphone). At this point the pilot initiated a turn and negative G dive to get away. As he turned the object fell in trail at what appeared to be about 3–4 NM. As he continued in his turn away from the primary object the second object went to the inside of his turn then returned to the primary object for a perfect rejoin.

D. Shortly after the second object joined up with the primary object another object appeared to come out of the other side of the primary object going straight down at a great rate of speed. The F-4 crew had regained communications and the weapons control panel and watched the object approach the ground anticipating a large explosion. This object appeared to come to rest gently on the earth and cast a very bright light over an area of about 2–3 kilometers. The crew descended from their altitude of 25,000 to 15,000 and continued to observe and mark the object's position. They had some difficulty in adjusting their night visibility for landing, so after orbiting Mehrabad a few times they went out for a straight in landing. There was a lot of interference on the UHF and each time they passed through a mag. bearing of 150 degrees from Mehrabad they lost their communications (UHF and interphone) and the INS fluctuated from 30 degrees to 50 degrees. The one civil airliner that was approaching Mehrabad during this same time experienced communications failure in the same vicinity (Kilo Zulu) but did not report seeing anything. While the F-4 was on a long final approach the crew noticed another cylinder-shaped object (about the size of a T-bird at 10M) with bright steady lights on each end and a flasher in the middle. When queried the tower stated there was no other known traffic in the area. During the time that the object passed over the F-4 the tower did not have a visual on it but picked it up after the pilot told them to look between the mountains and the refinery.

E. During daylight the F-4 crew was taken out to the area in a helicopter where the object apparently had landed. Nothing was noticed at the spot where they thought the object landed (a dry lake bed) but as they circled off to the west of the area they picked up a very noticeable beeper signal. At the point where the return was the loudest was a small house with a garden. They landed and asked the people within if they had noticed anything strange last night. The people talked about a loud noise and a very bright light like lightning. The aircraft and area where the object is believed to have landed are being checked for possible radiation.

More information will be forwarded when it becomes available.

Assessment: "Outstanding Report"
Equally as fascinating as the report itself was a form attached to the basic information given in the message. Titled, "Defense Information Report Evaluation," it was an assessment

of the quality of the Iran sighting details as determined by the Defense Intelligence Agency, a military version of the CIA which deals with foreign military intelligence. The form indicated in checked boxes that the reliability of information was "Confirmed by other sources," that the value of information was "High (Unique, Timely, and of Major Significance)," and that the utility of information was "Potentially Useful." The form added in the "Remarks" section:

> An outstanding report. This case is a classic which meets all the criteria necessary for a valid study of the UFO phenomenon:
>
> a) The object was seen by multiple witnesses from different locations (i.e., Shamiran, Mehrabad, and the dry lake bed) and viewpoints (both airborne and from the ground).
>
> b) The credibility of many of the witnesses was high (an Air Force general, qualified aircrews, and experienced tower operators).
>
> c) Visual sightings were confirmed by radar.
>
> d) Similar electromagnetic effects (EME) were reported by three separate aircraft.
>
> e) There were physiological effects on some crew members (i.e., loss of night vision due to the brightness of the object).
>
> f) An inordinate amount of maneuverability was displayed by the UFOs.

Judging from the comments by the DIA, the Iranian UFO chase was undoubtedly one of the premier UFO encounters in the history of the subject. A highly advanced vehicle, performing well beyond our present-day capabilities, created fits for the American-equipped Iranian Air Force. That the blackouts of the missile firing control panel, just before the pilot was about to launch his air-to-air missile, could be attributed to a mechanical fault seems beyond what sheer odds would allow. That an instrumentation blackout should occur on *two separate F-4 aircraft* as they were chasing a UFO is even more unlikely. The incidents described are such that to merely dismiss the report as unsupportive of UFO reality, which we anticipate will happen from some quarters, borders on the absurd.

Unfortunately, as in many other sightings we've discussed, while it has been stated in the Iranian message that "more information will be forwarded when it becomes available," such information has not been made available to the public. Reliable sources within the government have told us that the Iranian case file was about one and a half inches thick, yet absolutely no admission to having this file has come from any government agency with a possible connection to the case.

Interview with a Pilot

Two more interesting details came to light. In the October 1, 1976, issue of the *Iran Times* from Washington, D.C., an apparent firsthand account from one of the pilots involved in the chase was published (based on a tape of the actual pursuit). It says:

> The tape of Imperial Air Force Lt. Jafari's reports to the control tower at Mehrabad airport was made available.
>
> The 23-year-old pilot told controllers that the UFO had doubled back on its pursuers, and he was in danger of being forced down.
>
> Jafari was piloting the first of two jet fighters which took off from Shahrokhi Air Base in Hamadan to investigate the object.
>
> The aircraft flew toward Tehran at over the speed of sound, and the pilot contacted Mehrabad control after he had made contact with the UFO. He said on seeing him coming, the UFO increased its speed.
>
> "It was half the size of the moon as seen from earth," he said. "It was radiating violet, orange, and white light about three times as strong as moonlight."

Although the pilot was flying at maximum speed, he could not catch the UFO up.

The control tower told the pilot to return to base if he was not able to get near. The pilot agreed to do so, but a moment later radioed, "Something is coming at me from behind. It is 15 miles away . . . now 10 miles . . . now 5 miles."

"It is level now, I think it is going to crash into me. It has just passed by, missing me narrowly. . . ."

The disturbed voice of the pilot was clear on the tape. He then asked to be guided back to base.

It was at this time that a second plane was ordered to take off. Flying over Shahre Rey, the pilot reported having seen the UFO and told the control tower that it had reduced speed.

The pilot said the plane was working well and he was preparing to fire missiles at the UFO. After a moment's silence he said he had seen a "bright round object, with a circumference of about 4.5 meters, leave the UFO." A few seconds later the bright object joined the mother craft and it flew away at many times the speed of sound.

The authenticity of the object, however, already confirmed by several control tower officials at Mehrabad and the two pilots, was further backed up Sunday night by eyewitness reports from the area. People in the vicinity reported having seen a "bright body" flit across the sky while others claimed to have seen "some bright thing" falling from the sky.

Extraordinary Event

It was only in 1981 that the Air Force revealed another bit of information regarding the Iranian case. Requests for information on the sighting, directed to the National Security Agency (N.S.A.), revealed that an article written by a Captain Henry Shields was published in a periodical called the *MIJI Quarterly*. Published four times a year, the *MIJI Quarterly* contains narrative summaries of all "meaconing," "intrusion," and "jamming incidents" (therefore, MIJI) and is published by the Headquarters Electronic Security Command at San Antonio, Texas.

In case one may wonder, "meaconing" is a classified Air Force term and we cannot provide a definition for it.

Captain Shields' article, titled "Now You See It, Now You Don't," was included in the third quarter 1978 issue (then classified "Secret") and detailed the Iranian case in a three-page summary. The lead-in to the article is particularly interesting:

> Sometime in his career, each pilot can expect to encounter strange, unusual happenings which will never be adequately or entirely explained by logic or subsequent investigation. The following article recounts just such an episode as reported by two F-4 Phantom crews of the Imperial Iranian Air Force during late 1976. No additional information or explanation of the strange events has been forthcoming: the story will be filed away and probably forgotten, but it makes interesting, and possibly disturbing, reading.

The article basically recounted the details given in the message to the DIA.

Here we have an important endorsement for the anomalous nature of the sighting. It is very likely that a significant portion of what happened in the aftermath of the pilots' experiences has been highly classified, so high that even the author of the *MIJI Quarterly* article could not obtain further data regarding the landing.

Evidence: Military Eyewitnesses in England

Michael Hesemann

In the last week of December 1980, something strange happened in Rendlesham Forest, a woods between RAF Woodbridge and RAF Bentwaters, two NATO air bases in eastern England.

Between December 27 and 30 there were several sightings of strange lights, a strange craft, and, according to some witnesses, even aliens. The British Parliament and Ministry of Defense officially dismissed the case, saying that it did not present a security problem. But rumors about it traveled through UFO circles, and almost immediately, UFO investigators were onto the story, interviewing witnesses and trying to obtain confirmation.

The case did have extensive evidence that supported witness claims. There was a radar report of an unidentified object. There were multiple eyewitnesses, most of them considered credible. There was a tape recording of one of the security officers talking to his men in the woods as they were investigating the lights one evening. And there was physical evidence, including ground indentations that corresponded to the legs the witnesses said they saw the craft standing on, and an unusual degree of radiation in the immediate area. Animals from nearby farms were also reported to have been frenzied at the time of the sighting.

The case has generated a great deal of controversy, in part because of the sensational claims of some of the eyewitnesses. One non-UFO explanation considered plausible by many people was a nearby lighthouse that sent out strong light beams. But deputy base commander Lt. Col. Charles Halt told reporters on a television program, *Strange But True*, "A lighthouse doesn't move through a forest, doesn't explode, doesn't change shape, doesn't send down beams of light."

In the article below, German ufologist and documentary filmmaker Michael Hesemann describes some of the evidence of this case, including Lieutenant Colonel Halt's official report.

It all began quite harmlessly at an English pub, during a night in the year 1975, when the Englishwoman Brenda Butler met a young American soldier Steve Roberts (pseudonym), a security officer of the U.S. Air Force. They became friends and at some time or other, Brenda told Steve about her passionate interest in UFOs. Steve had heard a lot about these mysterious alien spaceships in the United States and knew comrades who had already had UFO experiences, mostly in service. And, when between 1975 and 1980 2 minor UFO incidents happened at Steve's base, the USAF-NATO base in Woodbridge he told Brenda about them. The UFO enthusiast received the news with great interest and

Steve asked her to keep the information confidential; otherwise, he would get into trouble with his superiors.

One day, in January 1981, Steve seemed to be anxious, as if he knew something he couldn't digest and about which he was not prepared to talk. But, on Brenda's continued insistence, he finally told her about something that was really very, very secret. Shortly after Christmas Day in the year 1980, a UFO had made an emergency landing in the Rendlesham Forest near Woodbridge. It had had technical problems and had landed at a clearance in the woods. He had been part of a security patrol which had observed the proceedings and had even witnessed an encounter between the base commander, Gen. Gordon Williams, and 3 small humanoid beings who came gliding out in a beam of light from the UFO.

Brenda was skeptical. But when one of Steve's colleagues told her that on the day in question, December 27, 1980, he had seen a whole convoy moving in the direction of Rendlesham Forest, Brenda began to believe the story. The soldier had said that he too, at that time, had heard that a UFO had landed only about a half a mile from the runway of the base. During the next few days, Brenda questioned the local people at the pubs and, again and again, got the confirmation that, at the time in question, strange lights had been seen in the sky. Then she decided to investigate more thoroughly. She joined forces with a local UFO researcher, Dot Street, who again brought in the UFO specialist and author Jennie Randles for advice. It turned out that Jennie herself was just then investigating the same story. In a roundabout way, she had come into contact with a radar operator of the RAF base Wharton at Norfolk. During the night of December 27, he had spotted an unidentified object in the Rendlesham Forest area on the radar screen.

That in itself would not have been particularly unusual. But a few days later, intelligence service officers of the U.S. Air

Force appeared at Wharton Air Force Base. The radar operators handed over the records in question to the Americans, on condition that they be told what had happened. The officers answered saying that a UFO had come down in the forest near Ipswich (in Suffolk), a metallic structured flying object of unknown origin. Security patrols that had come close to the object had reported that their motors had stopped running suddenly. They were forced to go on foot the rest of the way. The object hovered a few feet above the ground and it had taken some hours before it could be started again. During this time, the crew, 3 small beings, had communicated with the base commander, Gen. Gordon Williams.

An incredible story, if the research team Brenda Butler, Dot Street and Jennie Randles had not, during their further researchers, come across more witnesses. The USAF security officer James Archer (pseudonym) saw mysterious lights in the forest on December 27, 1980, at about 2:00 A.M. He reported this and was ordered to go to the forest together with 2 colleagues to see what was happening there. When the 2 MPs approached the lights, their radios stopped functioning. Finally they saw a *"triangular thing standing on legs."* It then lifted off and hovered above the forest ground. The landing legs had left impressions in the ground. Archer saw something in the spaceship which he took to be a robot because it was *"not human."* According to the commander of the security police at Woodbridge, Sgt. Adrian Bustinza, after Archer's first report a second patrol consisting of 2 cars with 2 men each went to the site of landing. Bustinza was himself in one of the cars, with the deputy commander of RAF Woodbridge, Lt. Col. Charles I. Halt.

When the 2 cars were near the site their motors also stopped running and they, too, had to walk the rest of the way. They then saw an object standing on 3 struts. It lifted off, flew a few feet above the trees and landed again. It moved up and down and had many lights in various colors. Photographers and cameramen were called for, and (Woodbridge) base commander Gordon Williams was informed. Steve Roberts affirmed that a number of security officers were present and photographs and films were taken, which were collected at once and sent for evaluation to the headquarters of the U.S. armed forces in Europe, the Main Air Force Base in Rhein, Germany. What the military men did not know was that at the same time thousands of local people observed the strange dancing lights in Rendlesham Forest, and saw the air force helicopter circling around the forest as well. In the neighboring area the animals started behaving strangely.

While the 3 UFO ladies were still continuing their research, an article that attracted much attention appeared in the popular scientific magazine *Omni* in America. The editor Eric Mischera quoted from an interview which he had had with Col. Ted Conrad, commander of the neighboring Bentwaters AFB. Conrad also confirmed the UFO landing, of which he was a witness. *"It was a large craft, mounted on tripod legs. It had no windows but was covered in red and blue lights. It definitely demonstrated intelligent control. After almost an hour it flew off at a phenomenal speed. It left behind a triangular set of marks evidently formed by the tripod legs. A later investigation proved the marks to be radioactive."* To hear that from the mouth of a high-ranking U.S. officer—Conrad was shortly after that promoted to the rank of General—was indeed a sensation. Even though Conrad had said nothing about the 3 extraterrestrials, Butler, Street and Randles could have hardly hoped for a better confirmation of the Woodbridge incident.

A Young Officer's Account

But that was not all. A young security officer, Airman Larry Warren, had told the United States UFO researcher Lawrence

Fawcett about a UFO landing in the forest at Rendlesham. According to Warren the incident had occurred on the night of December 29, 1980, a date also named by Col. Conrad, which suggests that during that short period at the end of December 1980, two landings had taken place in the same area. Warren was at this time stationed at the neighboring air force base in Bentwaters as part of the NATO exchange program. During the night of December 29, he and a few other security officers had driven in a jeep out into the countryside.

Once outside the base, Warren noticed that animals, mostly deer and rabbits, came running out of the forest as if in panic. They drove along a road into the Rendlesham woods until suddenly the motor stopped running. They got out and walked onwards, during which Warren saw a convoy leaving the base and coming towards the forest. Already at that distance he could hear the voices and noises of the radio apparatus, soon, however, to be drowned by the noisy sound of a helicopter flying over their heads. Then a group of other military personnel came, amongst them some British officers. One man in the group started shouting out loudly and hysterically and ran away. Warren had the feeling that *"World War III had just broken out."* Then he, too, saw the object. It was about 45 feet in diameter, hovered above the ground and looked like a *"transparent aspirin tablet."* It was pulsating slightly. Warren saw that a whole group of cameras was directed at the disc and that security officers were standing around at a respectful distance. He heard a voice, probably that of the pilot of the helicopter, saying over the radio *"It's coming now!"* They all looked up and saw a red object directly above them.

It was a bright red light that hovered for a short period above the "aspirin tablet" and then exploded in a rain of colors. For a moment all were blinded. When they recovered, they saw before them a big dome-shaped craft. Warren and few of his colleagues decided to get closer to the object. But when they had approached it so closely that they could almost touch it, a ray of green light shot out of the UFO and Warren lost consciousness. He came to again in the barracks. The mud from the forest expedition was still clinging to his boots and trousers. The next morning, Warren and his companions were called to see the base commander. They were told that they should under no circumstances tell the public about anything they had seen, for it was all put under extreme secrecy. . . .

Another Witness

Another witness, Sgt. John Burroughs, confirmed certain elements of Warren's story. He told me in an on-camera interview:

> Since something was seen in the second night, on the third night we decided to go back. When we got out there they already had people in the woods and stuff had already happened. They'd already spotted some stuff and they were following some stuff. We were held up for a while at a point before we were allowed to go any further. Eventually I met up with the people already out there and then I saw some blue lights in the sky, flying around, beaming stuff on the ground. The main object had landed some distance away. The impression I got from seeing it at this distance was that it almost looked like a huge Christmas display out there in the woods. Like different colored lights doing different colored things. Another thing I can tell you is that everything seemed to have a kind of slow motion effect. It seemed like things were happening somehow slower.

> Sgt. Adrian Bustinza and I at one point towards the very end saw the object in the distance seem to get closer and he and I started running towards it. As we were running, he went down to the ground, and later he claimed that something held him to the ground. I remember getting very close to something and suddenly remember standing in an open field and the thing was done. I don't remember anything

that happened, but there are people who said I jumped on top of the object—but I don't remember that.

Commander Halt's Report

Lawrence Fawcett applied to the Pentagon for information regarding this incident citing the Freedom Of Information Act and was given a report written about the incident by the vice-commander of Woodbridge, Lt. Com. Charles I. Halt. This report alone suffices to make the Rendlesham incident one of the strongest proofs for the existence of UFOs. Therein it says:

1. Early in the morning of 27 December, 1980, (approximately 3:00 A.M.), two USAF security police patrolmen saw unusual lights outside the back gate at RAF Woodbridge. Thinking an aircraft might have crashed or have been forced down, they called for permission to go outside the gate to investigate. The on-duty flight chief responded and allowed three patrolmen to proceed on foot. The individuals reported seeing a strange glowing object in the forest. The object was described as being metallic in appearance and triangular in shape, approximately 2 to 3 meters across the base and approximately 2 meters high. It illuminated the entire forest with a white light. The object itself had a pulsing red light on top and a bank(s) of blue lights underneath. The object was hovering or on legs. As the patrolmen approached the object it maneuvered through the trees and disappeared. At this time the animals on a nearby farm went into a frenzy. The object was briefly sighted approximately an hour later near the back gate.

2. The next day, three depressions 1½ inches deep and 7 inches in diameter were found where the object had been sighted on the ground. The following night, (29 Dec 80) the area was checked for radiation. Beta/gamma readings of 0.1 milliroentgens were recorded with peak readings in the three depressions, and near the center of the triangle formed by the depressions. A nearby tree had moderate (.05–.07) readings on the side of the tree towards the depressions.

3. Later in the night a red sun-like light was seen through the trees. It moved about and pulsed. At one point it appeared to throw off glowing particles and then broke into five separate white objects and then disappeared. Immediately thereafter three star-like objects were noticed in the sky, two objects in the north and one in the south, all of which were about 10° off the horizon. The objects moved rapidly in sharp angular movements and displayed red, green and blue lights. The objects to the north appeared to be elliptical, through an 8–12 power lens. They then turned to full circles. The objects to the north remained in the sky for an hour or more. The object to the south was visible for two or three hours and beamed down a stream of light from time to time. Numerous individuals, including the undersigned, witnessed the activities in paragraphs 2 and 3.

A Recording of the Incident

Col. Halt is even today prepared to confirm without any reservations the contents of his report. Besides that, an audiotape has been released in which he describes his observations before and after the landing:

> Voice: 1:48 A.M.: *"We're hearing very strange sounds out of the farmer's barnyard animals. They are very, very active, making an awful lot of noise . . . You saw a light? Slow down. Where?"*

> Halt: *"I see it too. What is it?"*

> Voice: *"We don't know, Sir."*

> Halt: *"I saw a yellow tinge in it, too. Weird. It appears to be maybe moving a little bit this way. It's brighter than it has been. It's coming this way. It is definitely coming this way! Pieces of it are shooting off. There is no doubt about it! This is weird!"*

> Voice: *"Two lights! One to the right and one light to the left!"*

> Halt: *"Keep your flashlight off. There's something very, very strange . . . Keep the headset on; see if it gets any . . . Pieces are falling off it again!"*

> Voice: *"It just moved to the right."*

> Voice: *"Yeah! Strange! Let's approach to the edge of the wood up*

there . . . OK, we're looking at the thing. We are probably about 2 to 3 hundred yards away. It looks like an eye winking at you. Still moving from side to side. And when you put the starscope on it, it's like this thing has a hollow center, a dark center, like the pupil of an eye looking at you, winking. And it flashes so bright in the starscope that it almost burns your eye . . . We've passed the farmer's house and across into the next field and now we have multiple sightings of up to 5 lights with a similar shape, but they seem to be steady now rather than a pulsating or glow with a red flash. We've just crossed a creek and we're getting what kind of readings now? We're getting 3 good clicks on the meter and we're seeing strange lights in the sky."

Halt: 3:05 A.M.: "At about 10 degrees, horizon, directly north, we've got 2 strange objects, er, half-moon shape, dancing about with colored lights on 'em . . ."

Voice: "They're both heading north. OK, here he comes from the south; he's coming toward us now, now we're observing what appears to be a beam coming down to the ground. This is unreal! . . ."

Halt: 3:30 A.M.: "The object to the south is still beaming down lights to the ground."

Halt: 4:00 A.M.: "One object still hovering over Woodbridge base at about 5 to 10 degrees off the horizon. Still moving erratic, with similar lights and beaming down as earlier."

The Government Is Hiding UFO Evidence

Lynn Picknett

Since the late 1940s—the beginning of the "modern" UFO era—many people have suspected that governments in general, but the U.S. government in particular, have hidden much of their knowledge about UFOs. And, in fact, revelations during the past three decades or so show just how extensive the cover-ups have been. In the United States, it was not only the air force that was investigating UFOs—so were several other government agencies, including the CIA, the NSA (National Security Administration), and even the FBI. With the passing of the Freedom of Information Act, many documents about the government's involvement in UFO research were made available to the public. Many people suspect that more documents remain to be found—or have been destroyed.

In the following article, British author Lynn Picknett, a

Excerpted from *The Mammoth Book of UFOs*, by Lynn Picknett (New York: Constable & Robinson Ltd., 2001). Copyright © 2001 by Lynn Picknett. Reprinted with permission.

former editor of *The Unexplained*, summarizes some of the available information about early UFO cover-ups.

The idea that world governments—in particular that of the United States—are engaged in a conspiracy to suppress the truth about UFOs is nearly as old as the phenomenon itself. The existence of such a conspiracy is an essential part of many key cases, such as the Roswell Incident and the Rendlesham Forest landing. And belief in the official cover-up is not confined to UFO enthusiasts: a survey by Ohio State University in 1995 found that 50 per cent of Americans believed that it was either "somewhat" or "highly likely" that their government is withholding information about UFOs.

The idea was initially popularized by Major Donald E. Keyhoe, the first writer on UFOs to reach bestseller status, and who produced a series of books in the 1950s and 1960s beginning with *The Flying Saucers Are Real* (1950). Keyhoe was a former Marine Corps pilot—and one-time aide to pioneer aviator Charles Lindbergh—who turned to writing after the Second World War. Keyhoe was first asked to look into the UFO mystery by the editor of *True* magazine, Ken Purdy, in 1949. Interestingly, Purdy's original brief, based on his own investigations, was that flying saucers were "a gigantic hoax to cover up [an] official secret."

As Keyhoe dug deeper into the mystery, using his contacts in the USAF, he became convinced that UFOs were extraterrestrial—and that the authorities knew it. In his next two books, *Flying Saucers from Outer Space* (1953) and *The Flying Saucer Conspiracy* (1955), he developed the twin themes that UFOs were alien spacecraft and that a "silence group" within the USAF was preventing this information from reaching the public.

Keyhoe went further in his self-imposed mission to expose the cover-up. In 1956 he founded the National Investigations Committee on Aerial Phenomenon (NICAP), which became the foremost of the civilian UFO research organizations. However, from the beginning an important part of NICAP's mission was to lobby Congress to open up the top secret files that Keyhoe and his associates believed were held by government organizations, in particular the USAF and the CIA.

Exercises in Misinformation

An essential part of Keyhoe and NICAP's argument was that official studies into flying saucers—which had all concluded that there was nothing to the phenomenon—were all exercises in misinformation designed to hide the truth from the public.

The flying saucer craze of the summer of 1947 had led to calls for an official investigation. The government charged the USAF with this task, and the first study, Project Sign, was launched in September 1947. Two years later it was redesignated Project Grudge, and in 1951 Project Blue Book, the name it retained until its closure in 1969. (In one of the frequent Kafkaesque episodes created by official secrecy, as the designations of military projects were themselves classified, ludicrously Project Sign used the "cover" name of Project Saucer when making public statements.) The team was based at Wright-Patterson Air Force Base at Dayton, Ohio.

The USAF studies, undertaken by a small team of underfunded, low-ranking officers, looked into reports by members of the public and issued periodic Press Releases on their findings. Perhaps predictably, while admitting that a small percentage of reports could not be explained by misidentification of conventional aircraft or natural phenomena, they concluded that there was no substance to the rumours of UFOs. Flying saucers didn't exist: it was official.

But to researchers such as Keyhoe, whose own investigations on the ground had convinced them of the reality of UFOs, this had to be a smokescreen.

What Keyhoe and other researchers suspected was that the real work was being done by other, more highly classified teams. We now know that he was correct: since the advent of the US Freedom of Information Act (FOIA) in 1974, previously classified documents have been unearthed that showed that other, secret studies *had* been undertaken, in particular by the CIA. UFOlogists were quick to use the FOIA to find out what the US military and intelligence agencies really knew about UFOs, the lead being taken by Ground Saucer Watch. One organization, Citizens Against UFO Secrecy (CAUS) was specifically created with this aim in mind.

The Twining Memo

One of the earliest official pronouncements on the flying saucer phenomenon was written in September 1947—although not made public until 1969. In a memo to his superior in USAF intelligence at the Pentagon, Lieutenant General Nathan F. Twining, after consulting with experts at the Air Technical Intelligence Center (ATIC) at Wright Field (later the Wright-Patterson Air Force Base), offered the conclusion that, "The phenomenon reported is something real and not visionary or fictitious." While this is an impressive endorsement—by USAF scientists, no less—that there was something to the UFO phenomenon, Twining's memo carried a sting in the tail for advocates of events such as the Roswell crash. It lamented the "lack of physical evidence in the shape of crash recovered exhibits which would undeniably prove the existence of these objects." As, according to the generally accepted reconstruction of the Roswell Incident, the crashed UFO and the bodies of its crew were sent to Wright Field for examination by ATIC, Twining's memo presents a serious difficulty. In mid-1948 Project Sign sent a report—known as the *Estimate of the Situation*—to the USAF Chief of Staff Lieutenant General Hoyt S. Vandenberg, which concluded that UFOs were real and that an extraterrestrial explanation was the most likely. Vandenberg disagreed, rejecting the report on the grounds that the evidence it gave did not support this conclusion. The report was destroyed, and the exact contents remain unknown. However, its existence was made known by Captain Edward J. Ruppelt, the Director of Blue Book between 1951 and 1953.

These two documents show that very soon after the first flying saucer reports, USAF scientists were not only taking the phenomenon seriously, but also considering an extraterrestrial explanation. Interestingly, it appears that they were the first to look to outer space for a solution, as the extraterrestrial hypothesis (ETH) did not become popular with the general public until the early 1950s.

The Robertson Panel

Perhaps the most significant of the secret studies was a CIA-sponsored group known as the Robertson Panel, after its chairman, the physicist Dr H.P. Robertson, who was then Director of the Defense Department's Weapons System Evaluation Group. Convened in January 1953, this was made up of five very eminent scientists, including the Nobel prize–winning physicist Dr Luis Alvarez (who later became famous as the originator of the "deep impact" theory of dinosaur extinction). The primary purpose of the Panel was not to pronounce on the reality or otherwise of UFOs—although it scathingly rejected any suggestion that they might be real—but to look at the implications of the *belief* in them.

It took five years for a summarized version of the Panel's report to be made public, and it was top of the list for UFOlogists when the FOIA became law in 1974, when the full report was finally obtainable.

The report concluded that UFO reports constituted "a threat to the orderly functioning of protective organs of the body politic" and recommended:

a. That the national security agencies take immediate steps to strip the Unidentified Flying Objects of the special status they have been given and the aura of mystery they have unfortunately acquired.

b. That the national security agencies institute policies on intelligence, training and public education designed to prepare the material defenses and the morale of the country to recognize most promptly and to react most effectively to true indications of hostile intent or action.

The report openly advocated the debunking of UFO reports in order to reduce public interest in the phenomenon.

The CIA's Concerns

However, matters are rarely clear-cut in the vexed world of UFO conspiracies. Opinions are divided about what the Robertson Panel reveals about the CIA's interest in, and knowledge of, UFOs. It confirmed—as Keyhoe and others suspected—that it was official policy to down-play and discredit UFO reports, but was this in order to suppress the truth about UFOs? In fact, this report—along with other declassified documents—shows that the CIA's main concern was in the social and psychological aspects of public belief in UFOs. The Panel had no hesitation in rejecting the reality of flying saucers—most damning of all was its statement that there was no physical evidence of their existence, again arguing against the Roswell Incident.

The Panel's greatest concern lay mostly with the consequences of the public's fascination with UFOs. In those nervy days of the early Cold War, there was a fear that the Soviet Union might flood America with bogus UFO reports, creating a "flap" that would tie up military communications and resources in advance of an attack. For this reason, a high degree of public interest in UFOs was evaluated as at best a nuisance, at worst a danger, and had to be discouraged.

For the same reasons, the CIA were interested in the mass psychology of UFO flaps. (There is an undeniable social aspect to waves of reports, whatever really lies behind them.) How did such waves start, and how could they be stopped? There was also the possibility that the phenomenon could be used in reverse—against an enemy.

A few months before the Robertson Panel study, in September 1952, the Director of the CIA's Office of Special Intelligence wrote a memo to Director Allen W. Dulles on the security implications of flying saucers, posing the question of "whether or not these sightings: (1) could be controlled, (2) could be predicted, and (3) could be used from a psychological point of view, either offensively or defensively."

Keeping the Public in the Dark

A month earlier a secret CIA briefing paper instructed that the Agency should prevent the public from finding out about its interest in UFOs, as otherwise it might appear to give credibility to the subject—proof that the Agency *did* keep its investigations secret (although not for the reasons given by advocates of the "UFO cover-up" theory).

As a result of the Robertson Panel's recommendations, the CIA effectively took charge of the USAF projects' policy. Not long after the Panel meeting, Captain Ruppelt and other USAF officers planned to go public with the Air Force data on UFOs—but the CIA stepped in and prevented them. Instead Blue Book was ordered to debunk the whole subject; if necessary by publicly ridiculing witnesses.

Three years after leaving Blue Book, Captain Ruppelt went into print, writing *The Report on Unidentified Flying Objects* (1956), which took an open-minded attitude to the phenomenon and even seriously considered an extraterrestrial explanation. However, he revised the book in 1959, explicitly rejecting the ETH. Many believe that the change was due to pressure from above. Ruppelt died of a heart attack a year later.

More suspicion centred on an Air Force Regulation (200-2) issued in August 1953—again probably as a result of the Robertson Panel recommendations—which categorized UFO reports by USAF personnel under intelligence activities and forbade them from talking about their experience to the Press or public. It also instructed that, at the discretion of the base commander, details of a sighting could be made public if it could be identified as "a familiar or known object". In other words, the public were to be given a distorted picture, and would only be told about reports that could be explained away.

The documents unearthed using the Freedom of Information Act generally showed that the CIA were open to the possibility that UFOs were extraterrestrial, but did not consider it likely. For example, a report by the CIA's Office of Special Intelligence in March 1949 referred to studies by several scientists and laboratories and noted:

> That the objects are from outer space or are an advanced aircraft of a foreign power is a possibility, but the above group have concluded that it is highly improbable . . . However, since there is even a remote possibility that they might be interplanetary or foreign aircraft, it is necessary to investigate each sighting.

In a similar vein, the head of the CIA's Weapons and Equipment Division wrote in a memo after the July 1952

Washington wave that, while he believed that all UFO reports could be explained conventionally if enough data was available, caution dictated that the Agency should continue to investigate reports in case they turned out to be of "alien origin".

So the declassified documents brought good and bad news for UFOlogists. They confirmed that the CIA—despite everything it had claimed previously—had been secretly interested in UFOs, had concealed that interest from the public, and that the public were being misled by the USAF investigations such as Blue Book. However, the reason for this was not to cover up what they really knew about UFOs. If anything, the documents reveal that the CIA were as puzzled as everybody else.

Chapter 2

Fact or Fiction?

UFOs Are Fiction

Evidence of UFOs Is Insufficient

Edward U. Condon

From 1948 to 1969, the U.S. Air Force conducted official investigations of UFO reports. Project Sign, followed by Project Grudge, and finally Project Blue Book collected nearly thirteen thousand reports from civilian and military witnesses in the United States and elsewhere and attempted to determine whether any were based on actual extraterrestrial sightings. The air force attributed more than 95 percent of the cases to normal causes, such as weather, misperceptions of the moon and planets, and misperceptions of ordinary aircraft. The remaining seven hundred were classified as unexplained.

Both public and military dissatisfaction with the air force role in the UFO investigations led to the establishment in November 1966 of an independent but government-funded study that, it was hoped, would shed some unquestionable and objective light on the UFO question. The University of Colorado agreed to host the study, which lasted two years and was headed by physicist Edward U. Condon. The study

Excerpted from *Final Report of the Scientific Study of Unidentified Flying Objects*, by Edward U. Condon (New York: E.P. Dutton, Inc., 1969).

was controversial from the start, with many people believing that committee members did not approach the topic with open minds. Nevertheless, its conclusions were significant. It concluded that there was little to be gained by further study of UFOs. The final report was presented to the government in early 1969, and by the end of the year Project Blue Book was shut down for good. The article that follows is excerpted from the report's opening chapter, "Conclusions and Recommendations."

We believe that the existing record and the results of the Scientific Study of Unidentified Flying Objects of the University of Colorado, which are presented in detail in subsequent sections of this report, support the conclusions and recommendations which follow.

As indicated by its title, the emphasis of this study has been on attempting to learn from UFO reports anything that could be considered as adding to scientific knowledge. Our general conclusion is that nothing has come from the study of UFOs in the past 21 years that has added to scientific knowledge. Careful consideration of the record as it is available to us leads us to conclude that further extensive study of UFOs probably cannot be justified in the expectation that science will be advanced thereby.

It has been argued that this lack of contribution to science is due to the fact that very little scientific effort has been put on the subject. We do not agree. We feel that the reason that there has been very little scientific study of the subject is that those scientists who are most directly concerned, astronomers, atmospheric physicists, chemists, and psychologists, having had ample opportunity to look into the matter, have individually decided that UFO phenomena do not offer a fruitful field in which to look for major scientific discoveries.

The Nature of Scientists

This conclusion is so important, and the public seems in general to have so little understanding of how scientists work, that some more comment on it seems desirable. Each person who sets out to make a career of scientific research, chooses a general field of broad specialization in which to acquire proficiency. Within that field he looks for specific fields in which to work. To do this he keeps abreast of the published scientific literature, attends scientific meetings, where reports on current progress are given, and energetically discusses his interests and those of his colleagues both face-to-face and by correspondence with them. He is motivated by an active curiosity about nature and by a personal desire to make a contribution to science. He is constantly probing for error and incompleteness in the efforts that have been made in his fields of interest, and looking for new ideas about new ways to attack new problems. From this effort he arrives at personal decisions as to where his own effort can be most fruitful. These decisions are personal in the sense that he must estimate his own intellectual limitations, and the limitations inherent in the working situation in which he finds himself, including limits on the support of his work, or his involvement with other pre-existing scientific commitments. While individual errors of judgment may arise, it is generally not true that all of the scientists who are actively cultivating a given field of science are wrong for very long.

Even conceding that the entire body of "official" science might be in error for a time, we believe that there is no better way to correct error than to give free reign to the ideas of individual scientists to make decisions as to the directions in which scientific progress is most likely to be made. For legal work sensible people seek an attorney, and for medical treatment sensible people seek a qualified physician. The nation's surest guarantee of scientific excellence is to leave the decision-making process to the individual and collective judgment of its scientists.

Scientists are no respecters of authority. Our conclusion that study of UFO reports is not likely to advance science will not be uncritically accepted by them. Nor should it be, nor do we wish it to be. For scientists, it is our hope that the detailed analytical presentation of what we were able to do, and of what we were unable to do, will assist them in deciding whether or not they agree with our conclusions. Our hope is that the details of this report will help other scientists in seeing what the problems are and the difficulties of coping with them.

If they agree with our conclusions, they will turn their valuable attention and talents elsewhere. If they disagree it will be because our report has helped them reach a clear picture of wherein existing studies are faulty or incomplete and thereby will have stimulated ideas for more accurate studies. If they do get such ideas and can formulate them clearly, we have no doubt that support will be forthcoming to carry on with such clearly-defined, specific studies. We think that such ideas for work should be supported.

Freedom to Explore

Some readers may think that we have now wandered into a contradiction. Earlier we said that we do not think study of UFO reports is likely to be a fruitful direction of scientific advance; now we have just said that persons with good ideas for specific studies in this field should be supported. This is no contradiction. Although we conclude after nearly two years of intensive study, that we do not see any fruitful lines of advance from the study of UFO reports, we believe that any scientist with adequate training and credentials who does come up with a clearly defined, specific proposal for study should be supported. . . .

Therefore we think that all of the agencies of the federal government, and the private foundations as well, ought to be willing to consider UFO research proposals along with the others submitted to them on an open-minded, unprejudiced basis. While we do not think at present that anything worthwhile is likely to come of such research each individual case ought to be carefully considered on its own merits.

This formulation carries with it the corollary that we do not think that at this time the federal government ought to set up a major new agency, as some have suggested, for the scientific study of UFOs. This conclusion may not be true for all time. If, by the progress of research based on new ideas in this field, it then appears worthwhile to create such an agency, the decision to do so may be taken at that time. . . .

The question remains as to what, if anything, the federal government should do about the UFO reports it receives from the general public. We are inclined to think that nothing should be done with them in the expectation that they are going to contribute to the advance of science.

This question is inseparable from the question of the national defense interest of these reports. The history of the past 21 years has repeatedly led Air Force officers to the conclusion that none of the things seen, or thought to have been seen, which pass by the name of UFO reports, constituted any hazard or threat to national security. . . .

No Evidence of Secrecy

It has been contended that the subject has been shrouded in official secrecy. We conclude otherwise. We have no evidence of secrecy concerning UFO reports. What has been miscalled secrecy has been no more than an intelligent policy of delay in releasing data so that the public does not become confused by premature publication of incomplete studies of reports.

The subject of UFOs has been widely misrepresented to the public by a small number of individuals who have given sensationalized presentations in writings and public lectures. So far as we can judge, not many people have been misled by such irresponsible behavior, but whatever effect there has been has been bad.

A related problem to which we wish to direct public attention is the miseducation in our schools which arises from the fact that many children are being allowed, if not actively encouraged, to devote their science study time to the reading of UFO books and magazine articles of the type referred to in the preceding paragraph. We feel that children are educationally harmed by absorbing unsound and erroneous material as if it were scientifically well founded. Such study is harmful not merely because of the erroneous nature of the material itself, but also because such study retards the development of a critical faculty with regard to scientific evidence, which to some degree ought to be part of the education of every American.

Therefore we strongly recommend that teachers refrain from giving students credit for school work based on their reading of the presently available UFO books and magazine articles. Teachers who find their students strongly motivated in this direction should attempt to channel their interests in the direction of serious study of astronomy and meteorology, and in the direction of critical analysis of arguments for fantastic propositions that are being supported by appeals to fallacious reasoning or false data.

We hope that the results of our study will prove useful to scientists and those responsible for the formation of public policy generally in dealing with this problem which has now been with us for 21 years.

Explanation: Research Balloons and Dummies

James McAndrew

The year 1997 marked the fiftieth anniversary of the Roswell incident, a UFO case that had become the touchstone for those who believed one or both of two things: that a UFO had crashed near the desert town of Roswell, New Mexico, and that the U.S. government was involved in a long-standing cover up to keep the truth about UFOs hidden from the public.

The Roswell story started with an official report released by the Roswell Army Air Field information officer to the *Roswell Record* on July 8, 1947, stating that the base had recovered a flying saucer. The newspaper printed the brief report with the huge headline "RAAF Captures Flying Saucer on Ranch in Roswell Region." Later the same day, General Roger Ramey went on the radio and stated that the report had been in error, that what had been recovered was actually a weather balloon. This pretty much put the case out of

Excerpted from *The Roswell Report: Case Closed*, by James McAndrew for the Headquarters of the United States Air Force (Washington, DC: U.S. Government Printing Office, 1997).

public light, for there were many other UFO reports that year, and one that had a mundane explanation was not remembered for long.

In 1978, however, UFO researchers Stanton Friedman and Charles L. Moore discovered some alleged firsthand witnesses who declared that it was indeed a UFO that had crashed at Roswell. Two years later, *The Roswell Incident* by Moore and Charles Berlitz provided detailed eyewitness accounts supporting the crashed saucer story. This book marked the beginning of Roswell's infamy. Over the next two decades a dozen or more books and numerous articles reported eyewitness testimony describing the crash debris, alien bodies, and government agents carting off these pieces of physical evidence to a secret site. Despite government denial and a spate of books countering the UFO testimony, the pro-Roswell books, combined with a general distrust of the government's openness, led many people to believe that the Roswell incident was the best evidence that flying saucers do exist.

In 1994, New Mexico congressman Steven H. Schiff demanded that government files be searched for any references to Roswell and UFOs. That same year, the air force did release a report, which asserted that the crash debris had been from a weather balloon, not a UFO. The following year, the government's General Accounting Office reported that all Roswell air base administrative records from March 1945 through December 1949 and all outgoing messages from October 1946 through December 1949 had been destroyed. To many people, this reinforced the belief in a cover-up.

As the fiftieth anniversary of the alleged Roswell crash approached, the air force scoured their files once more, looking for any additional evidence that might explain the incident. This research, plus their examination of the other evidence that seemed to support a UFO crash, resulted in a "final" report providing extensive detail showing that the debris was undoubtedly the remains of a research balloon and that the recovered "alien bodies" were actually research dummies. The report was not accepted by many UFO researchers, but others agreed with the air force—that with this report, authored by Captain James McAndrew, the Roswell case was closed. The following article is excerpted from the 1997 report.

From 1947 until the late 1970s, the Roswell Incident was essentially a non-story. The reports that existed contain only descriptions of mundane materials that originated from the Project MOGUL[1] balloon train—"tinfoil, paper, tape, rubber, and sticks." The first claim of "bodies" appeared in the late 1970s, with additional claims made during the 1980s and 1990s. These claims were usually based on anecdotal accounts of second- and third-hand witnesses collected by UFO proponents as much as 40 years after the alleged incident. The same anecdotal accounts that referred to bodies also described massive field operations conducted by the U.S. military to recover crash debris from a supposed extraterrestrial spaceship. . . .

The "Crash Sites"

From 1947 until the late 1970s, the Roswell Incident was confined to one alleged crash site. This site, located on the Foster Ranch approximately 75 miles northwest of the city of Roswell, was the actual landing site of a Project MOGUL balloon train in June 1947. The MOGUL landing site is referred to in popular Roswell literature as the "debris field."

1. Project MOGUL was a government program that used large research balloons.

In the 1970s, the 1980s and throughout the 1990s, additional witnesses came forward with claims and descriptions of two other alleged crash sites. One of these sites was supposedly north of Roswell, the other site was alleged to have been approximately 175 miles northwest of Roswell in an area of New Mexico known as the San Agustin Plains. What distinguished the two new crash sites from the original debris field were accounts of alien bodies. . . .

Common Threads

Careful examination of the testimony revealed that primary witnesses of the two "crashed saucer" locations contained descriptions common to both. These areas of commonality contained both general and detailed characteristics. However, before continuing, the accounts were carefully examined to determine if the testimony related by individual witnesses were of their own experiences and not a recitation of information given by other persons. While many aspects of the remaining accounts were judged to be similar, other aspects were found to be significantly different. The accounts on which the analysis is based were determined, in all likelihood, to have been independently obtained or observed by the witnesses.

General Similarities. The testimony presented for both crash sites generally followed the same sequence of events. The witnesses were in a rural and isolated area of New Mexico. In the course of their travels in this area, they came upon a crashed aerial vehicle. The witnesses then proceeded to the area of the crash to investigate and at some distance they observed strange looking "beings" that appeared to be crewmembers of the vehicle. Soon thereafter, a convoy of military vehicles and soldiers arrived at the site. Military personnel allegedly instructed the civilians to leave the area and forget what they had seen. As the witnesses left the area, the military personnel commenced with a recovery operation of the crashed aerial vehicle and "crew."

Detailed Similarities. Along with general similarities in the testimonies, there also existed a substantial amount of similar detailed descriptions of the "aliens," and the military vehicles and procedures allegedly used to recover them.

The first obvious similarity was the descriptions of the aliens. Mr. Gerald Anderson, an alleged witness of events at the site 175 miles northwest of Roswell, recalled, "I thought they were plastic dolls." Mr. James Ragsdale, an alleged witness of the site north of Roswell, stated, "They were using dummies in those damned things." Another alleged witness to a "crash" north of Roswell, Frank J. Kaufman, recalled that there was "talk" that perhaps an "experimental plane with dummies in it" was the source of the claims.

Additional similarities were also noted. Mr. Vern Maltais, a secondhand witness of the site 175 miles northwest of Roswell, described the hands of the "aliens" as, "They had four fingers." Anderson characterized the hands as, "They didn't have a little finger." He also described the heads of the aliens as "completely bald" while Maltais described them as "hairless." The uniforms of the aliens were independently described by Anderson as "one-piece suits . . . a shiny silverish-gray color" and by Maltais as "one-piece and gray in color." The date of this event was also not precisely known. Maltais recalled that it may have occurred "around 1950" and another secondhand witness, Alice Knight stated, "I don't recall the date."

Witnesses of different sites also used the terms "wrecker" and "six-by-six" when they described the military vehicles present at the different recovery sites. One witness described seeing a "medium sized Jeep/truck" and another witness described seeing a "weapons carrier" (a weapons carrier is a mid-sized Jeep-type truck).

The Research Profile

When the general and specific similarities were combined, a profile emerged describing the event or activity that might have been observed. The profile, which contains elements common to at least two, and in some cases, all of the accounts, established a set of criteria used to determine what the witnesses may have observed. The profile is as follows:

a. An activity that, if viewed from a distance, would appear unusual.

b. An activity of which the exact date is not known.

c. An activity that took place in two rural areas of New Mexico.

d. An activity that involved a type of aerial vehicle with dolls or dummies that had four fingers, were bald, and wore one-piece gray suits.

e. An activity that required recovery by numerous military personnel and an assortment of vehicles that included a wrecker, a six-by-six, and a weapons carrier.

Based on this profile, research was begun to identify events or activities with these characteristics. Due to the location of the sites, attention was focused on Roswell Army Air Base (AAF), renamed Walker Air Force Base (AFB) in 1948, White Sands Missile Range and Holloman AFB, N.M. The aerial vehicles assigned or under development at these facilities were aircraft, missiles, remotely-piloted drones, and high altitude balloons. The operational characteristics and areas where these vehicles flew were researched to determine if they played a role in the events described by the witnesses. . . .

High Altitude Research Balloons. The only vehicles not yet evaluated as a possible source of the accounts were high altitude research balloons. Previous reviews of early research balloon flight records revealed that trajectories of high altitude balloons were, at times, unpredictable and did not usually remain over Holloman AFB or White Sands Missile Range. Many of the scientific payloads required recovery so the data collected during flight could be returned to the laboratory for analysis. These characteristics seemed to fit at least some of the research profile. Atmospheric sampling apparatus or weather instruments, the typical payload of many high altitude balloons, could hardly have been mistaken for space aliens. A careful examination of the instruments carried aloft by the high altitude balloons revealed that one unique project used a device that very likely could be mistaken for an alien—an anthropomorphic dummy.

An anthropomorphic dummy is a human substitute equipped with a variety of instrumentation to measure effects of environments and situations deemed too hazardous for a human. These abstractly human dummies were first used in New Mexico in May 1950, and have been used on a continuous basis since that time. . . .

High Altitude Balloon Dummy Drops

From 1953 to 1959, anthropomorphic dummies were used by the U.S. Air Force Aero Medical Laboratory as part of the high altitude aircraft escape projects HIGH DIVE and EXCELSIOR. The object of these studies was to devise a method to return a pilot or astronaut to earth by parachute, if forced to escape at extreme altitudes.

Anthropomorphic dummies were transported to altitudes up to 98,000 feet by high altitude balloons. The dummies were then released for a period of free-fall while body movements and escape equipment performance were recorded by a variety of instruments. Forty-three high altitude balloon flights carrying 67 anthropomorphic dummies were launched and recovered throughout New Mexico between June 1954 and February 1959. Due to prevailing wind conditions, operational factors and ruggedness of the terrain, the majority of dummies impacted outside the confines of military reservations in eastern New Mexico, near Roswell, and in areas surrounding the Tularosa Valley in south central New Mexico. Additionally, 30 dummies were dropped by aircraft over White Sands Proving Ground, N.M. in 1953. In 1959, 150 dummies were dropped by aircraft over Wright-Patterson AFB, Ohio (possibly accounting for alleged alien "sightings" at that location). A number of these launch and recovery locations were in the areas where the "crashed saucer" and "space aliens" were allegedly observed.

Following the series of dummy tests, a human subject, test pilot Capt. Joseph W. Kittinger, Jr., now a retired Colonel, made three parachute jumps from high altitude balloons. Since free-fall tests from these unprecedented altitudes were extremely hazardous, they could not be accomplished by a human until a rigorous testing program using anthropomorphic dummies was completed.

Dummy Drop Procedures

For the majority of the tests, dummies were flown to altitudes between 30,000 and 98,000 feet attached to a specially designed rack suspended below a high altitude balloon. On several flights the dummies were mounted in the door of an experimental high altitude balloon gondola. Upon reaching the desired altitude, the dummies were released and free-fell for several minutes before deployment of the main parachute.

The dummies used for the balloon drops were outfitted with standard equipment of an Air Force aircrew member. This equipment consisted of a one-piece flightsuit, olive drab, gray (witnesses had described seeing aliens in gray one-piece suits) or fuchsia in color, boots, and a parachute pack. The dummies were also fitted with an instrumentation kit that contained accelerometers, pressure transducers, an ocscillograph, and a camera to record movements of the dummy during free-fall.

Recoveries of the test dummies were accomplished by personnel from the Holloman AFB Balloon Branch. Typically, eight to twelve civilian and military recovery personnel arrived at the site of an anthropomorphic dummy landing as soon as possible following impact. The recovery crews operated a variety of aircraft and vehicles. These included a wrecker, a six-by-six, a weapons carrier, and L-20 observation and C-47 transport aircraft—the exact vehicles and aircraft described by the witnesses as having been present at the crashed saucer locations. On one occasion, just southwest of Roswell, a HIGH DIVE project officer, 1st Lt. Raymond A. Madson, even conducted a search for dummies on horseback.

To expedite the recoveries, crews were prepositioned with their vehicles along a paved highway in the area where impact was expected.

On a typical flight the dummies were separated from the balloon by radio command and descended by parachute. Prompt recovery of the dummies and their suspension racks, which usually did not land in the same location resulting in extensive ground and air searches, was essential for researchers to evaluate information collected by the instrumentation and cameras. To assist the recovery personnel, a variety of methods were used to enhance the visibility of the dummies: smoke grenades, pigment powder, and brightly colored parachute canopies. Also, recovery notices promising a $25 reward were taped to an exposed portion of a dummy. Local newspapers and radio stations were contacted when equipment was lost.

Despite these efforts, the dummies were not always recovered immediately; one was not found for nearly three years and several were not recovered at all. When they were found, the dummies and instrumentation were often damaged from impact. Damage to the dummies included loss of heads, arms, legs and fingers. This detail, dummies with missing fingers, appears to satisfy another element of the research profile—aliens with only four fingers.

What may have contributed to a misunderstanding if the dummies were viewed by persons unfamiliar with their intended use, were the methods used by Holloman AFB personnel to transport them. The dummies were sometimes transported to and from off-range locations in wooden shipping containers, similar to caskets, to prevent damage to fragile instruments mounted in and on the dummy. Also, canvas military stretchers and hospital gurneys were used (a procedure recommended by a dummy manufacturer) to move the dummies in the laboratory or retrieve dummies in the field after a test. The first 10 dummy drops also utilized black or silver insulation bags, similar to "body bags" in which the dummies were placed for flight to guard against equipment failure at low ambient temperatures of the upper atmosphere.

On one occasion northwest of Roswell, a local woman unfamiliar with the test activities arrived at a dummy landing site prior to the arrival of the recovery personnel. The woman saw what appeared to be a human embedded head first in a snowbank and became hysterical. The woman screamed, "He's dead!, he's dead!"

It now appeared that anthropomorphic dummies dropped by high altitude balloons satisfied the requirements of the research profile. However, the review of high altitude balloon operations revealed what appeared to be explanations for some other sightings of odd objects in the deserts and skies of New Mexico.

Balloon Operations

Research has shown that many high altitude balloons launched from Holloman AFB, N.M., were recovered in locations, and under circumstances, that strongly resemble those described by UFO proponents as the recovery of a "flying saucer" and "alien" crew. When these descriptions were carefully examined, it was clear that they bore more than just a resemblance to Air Force activities. It appears that some were actually distorted references to Air Force personnel and equipment engaged in scientific study through the use of high altitude balloons.

Since 1947, U.S. Air Force research organizations at Holloman AFB, N.M., have launched and recovered approximately 2,500 high altitude balloons. The Air Force organization that conducted most of these activities, the Holloman Balloon Branch, launched a wide range of sophisticated, and from most perspectives, odd looking equipment into the stratosphere above New Mexico. In fact, the *very first* high altitude data gathering balloon flight launched from Alamogordo Army Airfield (now Holloman AFB), N.M., on June 4, 1947, was found by the rancher and was the first of many unrelated events now collectively known as the "Roswell Incident."

The Balloons

In 1946, as a result of research conducted for project MOGUL, Charles B. Moore, a New York University graduate student working under contract for the U.S. Army Air Forces, made a significant technological discovery: the use of polyethylene for high altitude balloon construction. Polyethylene is a lightweight plastic that can withstand stresses of a high altitude environment that differed drastically from, and greatly exceeded, the capabilities of standard rubber weather balloons used previously. Moore's discovery was a breakthrough in technology. For the first time, scientists were able to make detailed, sustained studies of the upper atmosphere. Polyethylene balloons, first produced in 1947 for Project MOGUL, are still widely used today for a host of scientific applications.

High altitude polyethylene balloons and standard rubber weather balloons differ greatly in size, construction, and utility. The difference between these two types of balloons historically has been the subject of misunderstandings in that the term "weather balloon" is often used to describe both types of balloons.

High altitude polyethylene balloons are used to transport scientific payloads of several pounds to several tons to altitudes of nearly 200,000 feet. Polyethylene balloons do not increase in size and burst with increases in volume as they rise, as do standard rubber weather balloons. They are launched with excess capacity to accommodate the increase in volume. This characteristic of polyethylene balloons makes them substantially more stable than rubber weather balloons and capable of sustained constant level flight, a requirement for most scientific applications.

The initial polyethylene balloons had diameters of only seven feet and carried payloads of five pounds or less. As balloon technology advanced, payload capacities and sizes of balloons increased. Modern polyethylene balloons, some as long as several football fields when on the ground, expand at altitude to volumes large enough to contain many jet airliners. Polyethylene balloons flown by the U.S. Air Force have reached altitudes of 170,000 feet and lifted payloads of 15,000 pounds.

During the late 1940's and 1950's, a characteristic associated with the large, newly invented, polyethylene balloons, was that they were often misidentified as flying saucers. During this period, polyethylene balloons launched from

Holloman AFB, generated flying saucer reports on nearly every flight. There were so many reports that police, broadcast radio, and newspaper accounts of these sightings were used by Holloman technicians to supplement early balloon tracking techniques. Balloons launched at Holloman AFB generated an especially high number of reports due to the excellent visibility in the New Mexico region. Also, the balloons, flown at altitudes of approximately 100,000 feet, were illuminated before the earth during the periods just after sunset and just before sunrise. In this instance, receiving sunlight before the earth, the plastic balloons appeared as large bright objects against a dark sky. Also, with the refractive and translucent qualities of polyethylene, the balloons appeared to change color, size, and shape.

The large balloons generated UFO reports based on their radar tracks. This was due to large metallic payloads that weighed up to several tons and echoed radar returns not usually associated with balloons. In later years, balloons were equipped with altitude and position reporting transponders and strobe lights that greatly diminished the numbers of both visual and radar UFO sightings. . . .

As early as May 1948, polyethylene balloons coated or laminated with aluminum were flown from Holloman AFB and the surrounding area. Beginning in August 1955, large numbers of these balloons were flown as targets in the development of radar guided air to air missiles. Various accounts of the "Roswell Incident" often described thin, metal-like materials that when wadded into a ball, returned to their original shape. These accounts are consistent with the properties of polyethylene balloons laminated with aluminum. These balloons were typically launched from points west of the White Sands Proving Ground, floated over the range as targets, and descended in the areas northeast of White Sands Proving Ground where the "strange" materials were allegedly found.

In 1958 the first manned stratospheric balloon flights were made from Holloman AFB. In 1960, balloon tests of components of the first U.S. reconnaissance satellite were also flown at Holloman AFB. In the 1960's, 70's, and 80's high altitude balloons were used in support of Air Force, and other U.S. Government and university sponsored research projects. Instrument testing of atmospheric entry vehicles for the National Aeronautics and Space Administration (NASA) space probes is one prominent example. . . .

The Surveyor (Moon), Voyager-Mars (Mars), Viking (Mars), Pioneer (Venus), and Galileo (Jupiter) spacecraft were tested by Air Force high altitude balloons before they were launched into space.

Viking and Voyager-Mars Space Probes. Examples of unusual payloads, not likely to be associated with balloons, were qualification trials of NASA's Voyager-Mars and Viking space probes. Both of these spacecraft looked remarkably similar to the classic dome-shaped "flying saucer."

In 1966–67 and 1972, eight of the UFO lookalikes were launched by the Balloon Branch from the former Roswell Army Air Field (now Roswell Industrial Air Center), N.M. The spacecraft were transported by Air Force balloons to altitudes above 100,000 feet and released for a period of self-propelled, supersonic, free-flight prior to landing on the White Sands Missile Range. While the origins of the "Roswell" scenarios cannot be specifically traced to these vehicles, their flying saucer-like appearance, and the fact that they were launched exclusively from the original "Roswell Incident" location, leaves an impression that perhaps these odd balloon payloads may have played some role in the unclear and distorted stories of at least some of the "Roswell" witnesses.

Explanation: Natural Earthlights

Paul Devereux

Is it possible that UFOs are not from outer space but are some form of naturally occurring phenomena? A number of researchers are convinced that when people see the mysterious lights they believe are UFOs, what they are really seeing are unusual but natural lights emitted by the Earth itself.

Witnesses over the centuries have reported many kinds of strange lights, some of which recur in the same location several days or nights in a row, or at regular intervals for many years. An example is the famous Marfa, Texas, mystery lights, dancing balls of light that have been occurring since 1883.

Geologists and other researchers have noticed that some of these mystery lights (which Paul Devereux, the author of this article, calls *earthlights*) are located near fault lines—places where the Earth's tectonic plates are fractured and under stress. The plates exert pressure and rub against each other creating electromagnetic energy that sometimes manifests as sparks or other light forms. This is called the piezo-electric effect. When someone strikes a flint against a stone to create a spark to start a fire, they are using this principle. Devereux says, "It is easy to see that enormous pressures in the earth at times of tectonic unrest, with huge bodies of crystal-bearing rocks crushing against one another, could easily produce enormous discharges of electrical energy." He theorizes that this electrical energy could sometimes appear to be a UFO.

In the early 1970s, a few researchers began to notice that some of the same geological characteristics present at the mystery lights were also present at many UFO sighting locations. In fact, the mystery lights themselves had some of the same characteristics as reported UFOs: Mystery lights appear in various colors, sometimes changing color and blinking on and off; they have various shapes, including ball, cigar, diamond, and tadpole forms; they may hover over a particular spot, dart quickly from one place to another, or travel in straight lines; they may appear to rise up out of the ground, fly over mountains, or hover over a lake or reservoir; they may appear and disappear abruptly or linger; they may be a single light or a group of several; they are sometimes visible from one direction but not another; they are sometimes accompanied by hissing, buzzing, or other sounds; and viewers sometimes experience physical side effects during or after seeing them, such as headaches, disorientation, and dizziness. These similarities inspired researchers to look for proof that UFOs might be forms of mystery lights rather than vehicles from outer space.

Paul Devereux, a British researcher, author, and lecturer, has studied earthlights for many years. He believes it is very possible that UFO witnesses are actually seeing earthlight phenomena. In the following article Devereux describes some of the research done by himself and other scientists that supports this idea.

The initial connection between geological factors and aerial phenomena considered specifically in the UFO frame of reference seems to have been made by a Frenchman, Ferdinand Lagarde, in a 1968 article in *Flying Saucer Review*. He made a study of a 1954 French UFO wave and noted that 37 per cent of low-level UFO sightings occurred on or close to geological faults, and that 80 per cent of the sighting locales were associated with faulting. . . . Further research showed a 40 per cent correlation between reported UFO incidence and fault lines. Lagarde commented: 'UFOs occur by preference on geological faults.' . . .

UFOs Occur in Similar Locations

By 1970 veteran American ufologist John Keel was making connections ahead of his time. His 1960s research had shown him that outbreaks of reported UFO events occurred in 'window' areas about 200 miles (322 km) across. These windows could also be part of larger geographical patterns, he felt. 'These are areas where UFOs appear repeatedly year after year,' he wrote [in his 1970 book *UFOs—Operation Trojan Horse.*]. Keel had grasped the key factor: there was a *geographical* dimension to the phenomena. He further noted that 'many . . . reports are concentrated in areas where magnetic faults or deviations exist'. He also made another remarkably pertinent observation, as we shall see: 'UFOs seem to congregate above the highest available hills in these window areas. They become visible in these centers and then radiate outward . . . before disappearing again.' Keel referred to a paper by Dr Martin D. Altschuler entitled *Scientific Study of Unidentified Flying Objects* and contributed to Colorado University in which he suggested that the UFOs resulted from rock friction—the piezo-electric effect. At the time Keel felt such an explanation was 'as far-out an explanation as visitors from Mars', and proceeded to view the window areas as places where interaction with some other level of reality was taking place.

But Keel did make direct associations between earthquakes and light phenomena, and at the same time felt that mechanisms existed to allow such an association to take place at a global level, quite apart from the small, window context. He quoted the case of 'a brilliantly illuminated object' that flashed across the northeastern United States at around 8.15 P.M. on 25 April 1966. It illuminated the countryside as it passed overhead, was seen by a great many witnesses, and came 'right on the heels' of a nationwide UFO wave in America. Keel probed further. He noted some events in Tashkent, Russia, around 5.23 A.M., 26 April, 1966. Galina Lazarenko, a Soviet scientist, was awakened by a flash of light so bright it lit up her room enabling her to see all the objects in it. The courtyard outside was similarly brilliantly illuminated. At the same moment, engineer Alexei Melnichuk heard a loud rumble followed by a bright flash while walking down a street. 'I seemed to be bathed in white light,' he recalled. Then the great Tashkent earthquake struck. It killed 10 people and made hundreds of thousands homeless. Many people who rushed out of their homes in panic reported seeing balloon-like glowing spheres in the air. Thinking globally, Keel realised that the Russian earthquake *was occurring at the precise time the fireball was arcing through American skies.* Furthermore, Keel discovered that Tashkent is at the same latitude as the northeastern United States. Unless this was a meaningless coincidence to end all coincidences, the likelihood is that under optimum circumstances, stimuli can occur within the planet resulting in simultaneous geophysical effects on a grand scale in different parts of the world.

UFOs Occur Near Fault Lines

Between 1972 and 1976 Andrew York and I made a part-time, multi-disciplinary study of the central English county of Leicestershire. We carried out extensive field and archive research, noting records covering over four centuries of unusual meteorology, seismicity, the locations of ancient sites, traditional gatherings, reported supernatural and ufological incidents, and related these to one another as well as to the county's geology to see what patterns, if any, might emerge. One that came up indicated that the faulting in the county, the areas where unusual seismicity and meteorology had been reported over the centuries, and the high incidence zones of reported UFO activity over a 25-year period, matched to a surprising extent. Although population distribution in the county confused this pattern to some extent, it certainly did not invalidate it. Leicestershire does not have a particularly exciting record of UFO activity, but we were able to perceive an underlying pattern indicating that those events which were reported did largely seem to relate to areas of faulting and certain kinds of exposed rocks over a period of years. One focus of UFO reports occurred round a curious hill called Croft Hill, some miles southwest of Leicester, which was a traditional gathering place down the centuries, for both religious and secular purposes. There is some evidence that it might have been the 'mesomphalos' of England and Wales, the central sacred hill, in Celtic times. It is an outcrop of granite and syenite and has two minor faults associated with it. A quarry is situated next to it. Another important aerial phenomena focus in the county is Charnwood Forest, an area of very ancient exposed rocks which has its own internal system of faults as well as faulting around its perimeter. It has been an epicentre for numerous recorded earthquakes and tremors down the years, including the 1957 event.

With this research, I started to become convinced that there had to be some sort of correlation between UFOs, strange weather and geological factors. Across the Atlantic, in North America, this correlation was given its most sophisticated presentation up to that time in *Space-Time Transients and Unusual Events* (1977) by Michael A. Persinger and Gyslaine F. Lafrenière. Both authors were from Laurentian University, Sudbury, Ontario, where Persinger is a professor of psychology and a research scientist.

UFOs Are Related to Tectonic Stress

The two Canadians made a study of UFOs and other anomalous, 'Fortean' events (named after Charles Fort [a famous early-twentieth-century researcher into unusual phenomena]), primarily in North America, and subjected them to various computer statistical analyses. Results indicated that the basic idea of 'window areas' was probably correct. For example, they tested unusual event clusters in the state of Illinois and found that there was a particular area that over the years exhibited a relatively larger incidence of unusual events than anywhere else in the state.

They considered many potential mechanisms that might be involved in the production of unusual events, particularly UFOs, ranging through stellar, planetary, solar and lunar influences on the Earth's geophysical systems, such as the geomagnetic field. The authors emphasised the vast energies contained within our globe: 'the existence of man upon a thin shell beneath which mammoth forces constantly operate, cannot be overemphasised.'

Such combined extra-terrestrial and terrestrial processes, Persinger and Lafrenière argued, would affect large areas of the globe, but might result in outbreaks of lights or unusual phenomena only in certain locations where geological stresses and other terrestrial factors were in a state of tension, ready to be triggered. (Tectonic stress waxes and wanes throughout the Earth's crust in many places every day, producing many small—sometimes imperceptible—tremors and only occasionally erupting as a major earthquake.) Fields of forces operating over very large geographical regions might focus in on just a few small areas due to particular seismic tensions, rock and mineral distributions and the like, creating localised conditions in which outbreaks of phenomena could take place that would be unlikely to occur if the background forces were evenly, widely distributed. . . .

Tectonic Stress Could Produce Strange Phenomena

Persinger and Lafrenière suggested that forces accumulating in a seismic area, perhaps over weeks or months, might produce a localised 'electric column'. Such a column would normally have a radius of between 10 and 100 feet (3–30 metres) but could, conceivably, have a radius of up to a mile under certain circumstances. The high electric field within such a column might cause a number of Fortean effects, and, if values reached sufficient levels, the air could become ionised, producing visible, glowing shapes in the air. The electrical column would move in keeping with the passage of tectonic stress along a fault or other line of weakness within the ground. A glowing ionised shape within the otherwise invisible column would thus appear to a witness to be flying a course over the landscape. The size of such a light and its height above ground would depend on the scale of the geological forces producing the column. (Strong earthquakes can certainly reach up to and disrupt the ionosphere. In the hour before the earthquake at Hilo, Hawaii, in 1973, for instance, radio transmission ceased due to the apparent 'disappearance' of the ionosphere!) This effect could work over bodies of water just as well as over land.

Some areas would experience this only on cycles measured in geologic time, thus to a human timescale phenomena appearing would seem to do so only randomly. Other areas would be more regularly prone to such flexing of tectonic forces, and so phenomena are more likely to repeat themselves within such locales on cycles that are within the range of human memory. Thus a 'window area' is recognised. This basic theory has come to be called the Tectonic Strain Theory (TST).

"UFOs" Can Occur Without Earthquakes

The two researchers pointed out that earthquakes themselves would not be necessary to produce such lights; indeed, a quake would release the stress being built up within rock and mineral bodies within the crust. A quake only occurs when rocks give way under the strain, otherwise the stress builds up and then relaxes, the massive pressures involved not actually triggering deformation of the Earth's crust. Persinger and other proponents of the TST have suggested, therefore, that lights might be associated with very small quakes, where only limited rock fractures have occurred. Such seismicity might not register sensibly to people over such locations of tectonic stress, and may, indeed, not even be recorded by the available network of instrumental monitoring.

The theory also allows for effects on the human witness of light phenomena. The electric column could affect the brain function of a witness standing within it while observing a lightform. This would allow the possibility of explaining 'exotic' UFO encounters where humanoids, abductions and short periods of amnesia are allegedly reported. Further, energy fields surrounding light phenomena may cause burning and radiation-like effects on witnesses, as well as on the immediately local physical environment. Such effects are reported from time to time in the UFO literature. . . .

A Study Shows Connection Between UFOs and Fault Lines

It seemed to me that we needed to close in on much smaller areas than had been attempted at that time in the North American studies to see if there really was an intimate connection between reported UFOs and faulting: while faulting was by no means the only geophysical aspect to take into account, it was fair to expect that faulting would frequently be a prominent factor in areas associated with light phenomena if the basic TST was correct. It was one important aspect of the pattern to check. Patterns that look convincing when brushed in with broad strokes, can, when examined at close quarters, break down. We were to find that in this case the opposite was to occur—it was to get stronger the closer we looked. We were in a fortunate position: Britain is a relatively small area, yet possesses 'amazingly enough, strata of every geologic period from the pre-Cambrian to the Quaternary' as one Japanese book puts it. Added to this, Britain is very well mapped both geographically and geologically (though there are still annoying gaps in the readily-accessible large-scale geological record), and it has active UFO research groups so a reasonable collection of reported UFO data takes place.

Even with these advantages, however, it proved surprisingly difficult to get an area that had a good set of UFO reports from which geographical locations could be accurately determined, and which also had sufficiently detailed geological maps to at least 1:50 000 (2 centimetres to 1 km) scale.

But our first 'test' was both obvious and easy—Warminster in Wiltshire. This small market town came into ufological prominence in the mid-1960s when a 'Thing' started to be seen in its local skies. People from all walks of life saw lights and cigar-shapes in the area. A local journalist, Arthur Shuttlewood, began to write colourful books on the matter, and UFO events reported at Warminster were regularly described in the UFO specialist journals (Warminster even had its own for a while), and the general press, too. Before long, UFO enthusiasts from all over Britain—and elsewhere—began to descend on the area to carry out 'skywatches' on nearby hills: Warminster had become one of the country's most celebrated 'ufocals'. Even the town's name derived from 'worm' which meant serpent or dragon in old English.

One of the key locations for UFO manifestation was Cley Hill, a mile or two to the west of Warminster. It was a chief 'window' according to Shuttlewood when I asked him at the time. A curious natural hill, it was also artificially earthworked in prehistoric times.

Data Supports the Earthlight Theory

For our research, we contacted Barry Gooding, a local ufologist who had kept a careful eye on the UFO reports over the years. He felt, like most serious ufologists, that the great majority of the supposed sightings were of aircraft lights, satellites and other misidentified mundane features. Furthermore, there had been a good deal of media 'hype' surrounding the Warminster Thing. Nevertheless, he was quite satisfied that there was *something* odd going on. He felt a certain percentage of the reports did refer to a real, but unexplained, phenomenon—an orange lightform that was seen to gambol around the local Warminster landscape. It came to be nicknamed 'The Amber Gambler' by the ufologists in the area. Gooding also had accounts from people who had seen lightforms in ball and ellipsoid forms apparently *entering the slopes of Cley Hill*. Other reports talked of lightbeams emerging from the ground, forming into balls of light and flying off.

Warminster looked an improbable candidate for the

earthlights theory because it was situated in chalk country (as demonstrated by the nearby Westbury White Horse chalk hill figure, for example) and such geology is usually tectonically stable. So there were unlikely to be many surface faults around. When the 1:50 000 scale geological map was consulted this was the case—there were only two recorded surface faults in the whole region of countryside around Warminster. But those two were right at Warminster itself! One fault goes immediately alongside Cley Hill and on through the town, while a shorter fault runs parallel to the first, close to Cley Hill. We had scored an unlikely bullseye.

Explanation: Venus

Bob Berman

Of all the UFOs reported, a significant number turn out to be sightings of the planet Venus. In the following article, Bob Berman comments on this tendency of even sky-knowledgeable people to confuse natural sky lights with UFOs. Berman is an astronomer, pilot, and author of *Secrets of the Night Sky.*

You'd think everyone could identify Venus. For backyard astronomers, recognition is automatic; it's as challenging as locating the moon. Yet most people are clueless about that dazzling "star"—some even grab the phone and report an Unidentified Flying Object.

Jimmy Carter did, while governor of Georgia. The Evening Star's brilliance so puzzled and concerned him that he alerted the State Police. And in World War II, a squadron of B-29s returning from a mission over Japan grew increasingly anxious about a bright light that seemed to follow them. They turned around and tried, unsuccessfully, to shoot down Venus.

Some years back, a survey named Venus as the single most common cause of UFO reports. Size-for-size, its light is far more intense and concentrated than moonlight, especially when at its very brightest, as it is during late February and early March. Its steady, non-twinkling glow makes it seem eerily unstarlike.

Moreover, when the Evening Star reaches peak brilliance in late winter, it remains out long after twilight, setting its dazzle against a black sky for an even more theatrical effect.

Police stations can count on "alien spacecraft" calls at this time of year. And some people regard observatories as official UFO Reporting Centers. I've received a couple of reports a month during peak-Venus periods, though my neighborhood probably gets more reports than most; it includes the flashback-prone Woodstock region.

When UFO Sightings Are Resolved

People have interesting reactions when their UFO sighting has been resolved. Many are excited to know that they've seen our neighboring planet, and they appreciate having their curiosity so decisively satisfied. But others sound disappointed. They seem to want to be invaded by aliens. Still others have heard of UFOs for decades and wish to amuse themselves by seeing an unambiguous example of extraterrestrial tourism.

When I lecture to astronomy groups—my favorite audiences—I usually ask how many have ever seen a UFO. I've continuously added to my informal survey, satisfying my bias that those who know the sky never encounter such things. To be honest, however, a couple of people in every group of 40 or 50 do report having viewed mystery lights. I once assumed that these were novices who hadn't yet seen things like bolides (exploding meteors) dramatically blowing themselves to bits. But no, many backyard astronomers give straightforward accounts of lights performing zigzags or other impossible aerobatics, sightings that seem to preclude all natural explanation.

It seems arrogant to dismiss some of these stories by sober and intelligent people. Yet I've been watching the skies for 40 years, and as an airplane owner I also do a fair amount of night flying, and I've never seen a UFO. Moreover, I've often witnessed high UFO-sensitivity, as when students excitedly point at a satellite or plane and nervously yell, "What the heck is that?"

To me, the best case against UFOs is that very few knowledgeable amateur astronomers who keep the heavens under nightly observation ever see such things. It also seems suspicious to me that these aliens are smart enough to get all the way here from Epsilon Eridani but wish to remain anonymous (since they're not landing on the White House lawn or even at the Green Party headquarters). Still they keep getting caught by earthbound viewers like incompetent cat burglars. And nobody ever catches them on a clear, focused videotape.

Then there are the hoaxes and pranks. A group of pilots from nearby Stormville Airport, here in rural upstate New York, admitted that they sometimes flew in formation at night with lights blazing, just because they loved to read the UFO reports in the paper the next day. Who knows how many other playful types are into such UFO mischief?

Amazing Venus

Though not an alien spacecraft, Venus still manages to do amazing things. For starters, it now briefly joins the sun and moon as the only natural objects that can cast shadows. It also joins the elite club of the moon and Mercury as the only celestial objects that assume crescent shapes to our eyes. (Venus's crescent gets absolutely fabulous during March, especially when viewed in twilight.) But its strangest feature may simply be that sometimes it can be easily viewed as both a morning and evening star simultaneously. This is a trick it only performs once in each of its eight-year repertory cycles. Venus goes around the sun 13 times while Earth simultaneously makes eight circuits, so these venusian shenanigans repeat almost precisely every eight years.

In late March [2001], then, Venus will readily appear just above the western horizon immediately after sunset, but also materialize in the eastern sky right before sunrise. It seems to be on both sides of the sun at the same time.

This nifty maneuver arises because Venus will scoot quite a bit north of the sun at inferior conjunction on March 30, letting it set later and rise earlier for Northern Hemisphere observers than the more southerly-sited sun. In just another three years, Venus will pass directly in front of the sun for the first time since 1882, visible from the eastern United States and Europe. I've been waiting for this transit of Venus since I was a kid (despite that I know it'll be cloudy in New York that morning).

That's just two inferior conjunctions away. This time, Venus misses the sun by quite a bit, which allows anyone with a setting-circle or computer-guided telescope to view Venus by day, continually, as it crosses over to become a morning star.

(Be careful. Don't "sweep" your scope near the sun while looking for it. You don't want to get a blast of full sunlight through the eyepiece, like I once stupidly did.)

During the last week of March, Venus will not only be at its most visible and its skinniest, but it may display for you its mythical ashen light—an eerie glow that diffuses through its clouds to illuminate some of its dark hemisphere. Venus is fabulously strange, even if it isn't a UFO.

Maybe observatories can simply play a recorded message that says that dazzling light is not from another planet. It is another planet.

Explanation: Delusion

Robert L. Park

One of the most common explanations for the many of the thousands of UFO reports made each year is simple delusion: No matter how observant people are, it's easy to be fooled under the right conditions. In the following viewpoint, physicist and UFO skeptic Robert L. Park reflects on his own UFO incident. Park teaches at the University of Maryland in College Park and is the director of the American Physical Society, headquartered in Washington, D.C.

In the summer of 1954, when I was a young Air Force lieutenant, I was sent on temporary assignment to Walker Air Force Base in Roswell, New Mexico, to oversee the installation of a new radar system. Late one night I was returning to the base after a weekend visit with my family in Texas. I was driving on a totally deserted stretch of highway. The sky was moonless but very clear, and I could make out a range of ragged hills off to my left, silhouetted against the back-

Excerpted from "Welcome to Planet Earth," by Robert L. Park, *The Sciences*, May/June 2000. Copyright © 2000 by *The Sciences*. Reprinted with permission.

ground of stars. Suddenly the entire countryside was lit up by a dazzling blue-green light, streaking across the sky just above the horizon.

The light flashed on and off as it passed behind the hills, then vanished without a sound. It was all over in perhaps two seconds. At the time, reported sightings of unidentified flying objects—UFOs—made the news almost daily. Indeed, the town where I was stationed, Roswell, was the hub of many such speculations. But I prided myself on being a skeptical thinker, and I had little patience for wacky ideas about flying saucers invading the earth.

In fact, I had a perfectly plausible explanation for the spectacular event I had just witnessed. Pale blue-green is the characteristic color of the light emitted by certain frozen free radicals as they warm up. A free radical is a fragment of a molecule, and one well-known variety of free radical is the so-called hydroxide radical—a water molecule that is missing one of its hydrogen atoms. Free radicals are energetically predisposed to reconnect with their missing parts, and for that reason they are highly reactive: ordinarily they do not stick around very long.

But if molecules are broken up into free radicals by radiation at low temperatures, the radicals can be frozen in place. Then, when the severed parts of the molecule are warmed up, they readily recombine to form the same kinds of stable molecules from which they originated. The energy that is liberated when hydroxide radicals recombine with hydrogen atoms to form water appears as blue-green fluorescence. It occurred to me that an ice meteoroid would gradually accumulate hydroxide radicals as a result of cosmic-ray bombardment. What I had had the good fortune to see just then, I reasoned, was a meteor plunging into the earth's upper atmosphere, where it warmed, setting off the recombination reaction.

A Saucer Appears

As I continued driving down the empty highway and crossed into New Mexico, I felt rather smug. The UFO hysteria that was sweeping the country, I told myself, was for people who don't understand science. Then I saw the flying saucer.

It was off to my left, between the highway and the distant hills, racing along just above the rangeland. It appeared to be a shiny metal disk, thicker in the center than at the edges, and it was traveling at almost the same speed I was. Was it following me? I stepped hard on the gas pedal of the Oldsmobile—and the saucer accelerated. I slammed on the brakes—and it stopped. Only then could I see that it was my own headlights, reflecting off a telephone line strung parallel to the highway. The apparition no longer looked like a flying saucer at all.

It was a humbling experience. My cerebral cortex might have sneered at stories of flying saucers, but the part of my brain where those stories were stored had been activated by the powerful experience of the icy meteorite. At an unconscious level, my mind was busy making connections and associations. I was primed to see a flying saucer—and my brain filled in the details.

Who has not "seen" an animal in dusky twilight that turns into a bush as one takes a closer look? But something more than the mind playing tricks with patterns of light is needed to explain why hundreds—by some accounts thousands—of people claim to have been abducted by aliens, whisked aboard a spaceship and subjected to some kind of physical examination, usually focusing on their erogenous zones. After the examination, the aliens are frequently said to insert a miniature implant into the abductee's body. Often the memory of an abduction has a dreamlike quality, and subjects can recall the details only under hypnosis.

Scientists themselves are not immune to such beliefs. In 1992 a five-day conference was held at the Massachusetts Institute of Technology to assess the similarities among various accounts of alien abduction. The conference was organized by John E. Mack, a Harvard psychiatrist, and David E. Pritchard, a prize-winning MIT physicist. Mack had been treating patients who thought they had been kidnapped by aliens. His treatment was to reassure them that they were not hallucinating but really had been abducted.

Pritchard, an experimentalist, was more interested in the physical evidence of the kidnappings, particularly the minuscule implants. The most promising candidate seemed to be an implant that abductee Richard Price said had been inserted midshaft into his penis. The implant, amber in color and the size of a grain of rice, was clearly visible. Under a microscope, what appeared to be fine wires could be seen protruding from it. What wonders of alien technology might be revealed by a sophisticated analysis of that diminutive device? Amid high expectations, the "implant" was removed and examined. The conclusion? It was not from Andromeda. Its origins were distinctly terrestrial: human tissue that had accreted fibers of cotton from Price's underwear.

It is hardly surprising that there are similarities in the accounts of people who claim to have been abducted by aliens. All of us have been exposed to the same images and stories in the popular media. My local bookstore stocks three times as many books about UFOs as it carries about science. Aliens stare at us from the covers of magazines and make cameo appearances in television commercials. As time goes by, the depictions become increasingly uniform. Any six-year-old can now sketch what an alien looks like. Popular culture is, in fact, undergoing a kind of alien evolution: each new creation by a filmmaker or sci-fi writer acts as a mutation, and the selection mechanism is audience approval. Aliens subtly evolve to satisfy public expectations.

The widespread belief in alien abductions is just one example of the growing influence of pseudoscience. Two hundred years ago, educated people imagined that the greatest contribution of science would be to free the world from superstition and humbug. It has not happened. Ancient beliefs in demons and magic still sweep across the modern landscape, but they are now dressed in the language and symbols of science: A best-selling health guru asserts that cancer can be banished from the body by the power of the mind. If anyone should doubt it, he explains that it's all firmly grounded in quantum theory. Inventors claim to have built perpetual-motion machines that circumvent the laws of physics. Educated people wear magnets in their shoes to draw "energy" from the earth.

Voodoo science is everywhere. But why? Perhaps the most endearing characteristic of Americans is their sympathy for the underdog. They resent arrogant scientists who talk down to them in unfamiliar language, and government bureaucrats who hide behind rules. Scientists, meanwhile, often look the other way when science is being abused, expecting bogus claims to self-destruct. But members of the public are often not in a position to distinguish between fabulous but verifiable phenomena, such as hermaphrodites and antimatter, and fanciful ones, such as touch therapy and astrology. It's up to the scientists to inform the nonscientists—and to remember how easy it can be to subscribe to erroneous ideas. Whenever I become impatient with UFO enthusiasts, as I often do, I try to remember that night in New Mexico when, for a few seconds, I, too, believed in flying saucers. . . .

Recent polls indicate that a growing number of people think the government is covering up information about UFOs. Nevertheless, it is easy to read too much significance into reports of widespread public belief in alien visits to earth. The late astronomer and science popularizer Carl Sagan saw in the myth of the space alien the modern equivalent of the demons that haunted medieval society, and for a susceptible few they are a frightening reality. But for most people, UFOs and aliens merely add a touch of excitement and mystery to uneventful lives. They also provide a handy way for people to thumb their noses at the government.

Explanation: Experimental Aircraft

Jim Wilson

The decades immediately following World War II were a time of suspicious rivalry between nations, particularly the United States and the Soviet Union. They were also a time of numerous UFO sightings. Could there be a connection?

Today, as more and more formerly classified documents have been released by both governments, it is clear that some UFOs were secret experimental or reconnaissance aircraft neither country wanted its rival to know about. The Stealth B-2 bomber is one of the more recent examples of aircraft that could easily be mistaken for a UFO. The dark triangular plane is nearly invisible to radar, and it was a craft unknown to most civilians until the late 1990s. The Soviet Union, too, had its secrets. In the fall of 1967, the crew of a Russian airliner claimed a UFO had hovered nearby and then disappeared. In fact, the USSR experienced an amazing wave of UFO sightings during 1967. It has only been since

From "The Secret CIA UFO Files," by Jim Wilson, *Popular Mechanics*, November 1997. Copyright © 1997 by *Popular Mechanics*. Reprinted with permission.

the USSR's collapse that the secrets have been exposed: At least some of those UFOs were illegal space-to-earth nuclear weapons or other experimental craft.

The following article comments on some of the U.S. secret aircraft that led to erroneous reports of UFOs. Jim Wilson is science editor at *Popular Mechanics*.

The Central Intelligence Agency says it has finally come clean about UFOs. To absolutely no one's surprise, it knew more than it ever let on.

"Over half of all UFO reports from the late 1950s through the 1960s were accounted for by manned reconnaissance flights," says Gerald K. Haines, a historian for the National Reconnaissance Office who studied secret CIA UFO files for an internal CIA study that examined the spy agency's involvement in UFOs through the 1990s.

Why Lie About UFOs?

Why lie about UFOs? "The Soviets could use UFO reports to touch off mass hysteria and panic in the United States and overload the U.S. air warning system so that it could not distinguish real targets from phantom UFOs," Haines says.

If Cold War hysteria seems to be a less than satisfactory explanation, perhaps it is because there really is more to the story.

Popular Mechanics has learned from nonclassified sources that the United States had a serious reason for wanting the public to keep believing that the strange lights in the sky were of unearthly origin. The government kept the UFO myth alive to disguise the embarrassing fact that during the hottest days of the Cold War, America's two most secret intelligence gathering assets—the A-12 and SR-71 spyplanes—

flew toward hostile terrain with the equivalent of cow bells dangling from their necks.

The deception of the public began in the early 1950s. It involved the then highly secret, and to this day little-known, A-12. If you think you saw an SR-71 Blackbird at an air and space museum, the odds are you were actually looking at an A-12. The idea for the plane was conceived in 1954 by CIA director Allen Dulles. The objective of this secret program, according to aviation historian Paul F. Crickmore, was to build a spyplane capable of flying higher and faster than the U-2.

The secret development program, which was originally called Project Aquatone, and then Gusto and then Oxcart, led to the first A-12 mockup. It became connected with UFO lore in late 1959 when, according to Crickmore, it was trucked from the famous Lockheed Skunk Works, in Palmdale, California, to Groom Lake, Nevada. (Also known to UFO enthusiasts as Area 51, this formerly secret test site is located about 100 miles north of Las Vegas, Nevada.) Hidden in the desert and surrounded by then active Atomic Energy Commission testing grounds, the A-12 mockup underwent a series of tests to determine and then reduce its ability to deflect and absorb radar signals. The CIA liked what it saw and ordered a dozen.

Lockheed had built what to this day is considered the most amazing aircraft of all time. But before it could fly, it needed engines that could propel the plane to Mach 3.2 and an altitude of more than 97,600 ft. In February 1962, Pratt & Whitney announced its already overdue J58 engines could not be delivered anytime soon. As an interim solution, they offered less powerful J75 engines that, according to Crickmore, would take the A-12 to about 50,000 ft. and a speed of Mach 1.6. CIA engineers accepted the offer after calculating that an A-12 equipped with a pair of J75 engines should be able to fly faster than Mach 2.

"In order to placate the directors who controlled the agency's purse strings, [Lockheed test pilot] Bill Park dived an A-12 to Mach 2," says Crickmore. "[It] relieved some of the high-level pressure on the design team." Without intending to, Park also opened a new chapter in UFO history.

Baffling Abilities

One of the features about UFO sightings that has consistently baffled the experts is their apparent ability to swoop downward, hover and then soar into the sky at impossible speeds.

Viewed head on, this is exactly how an A-12 or an SR-71— its J58-powered successor—appears to move at times during a normal flight. The maneuver is called a "dipsy doodle."

Col. Richard H. Graham, who commanded the U.S. Air Force 9th Strategic Reconnaissance Wing and has written a history of the SR-71 titled *SR-71 Revealed*, recently explained the dipsy doodle to *Popular Mechanics*. The pilot begins by climbing to about 30,000 ft. with the afterburners glowing. At about 33,000 ft., with the plane at Mach .95, he noses the aircraft over. Heading down at a pitch as great as 30°, the plane falls as fast as 3000 ft. per minute. After 10 to 20 seconds, the pilot pulls out of the dive, then accelerates skyward at more than twice the speed of sound.

There is one more very UFO-like characteristic of the SR-71: The glow of its exhaust periodically turns green.

The SR-71 burns fuel modified to withstand high temperatures. It doesn't light easily. "One early 'hiccup' was ignition," Crickmore recalls. "The [J58] engine would not start no matter what procedure was tried."

Eventually the problem was solved by the introduction of a chemical that explodes on contact with the atmosphere. Graham says it must be introduced into the engine when it is started, and it also kicks-in the afterburners. This happens after each aerial refueling, which, given the SR-71's enormous thirst, is quite often. Each time, it produces another image that could be misinterpreted as a UFO—flashing colored lights.

The green flash and distinctive dipsy doodle can be spotted from miles away. Observing the pattern created by these strange sights provides a map to the SR-71's target area, giving those on the ground enough time to hide whatever the spyplane has been sent to photograph.

Curiously, the ebb and flow of UFO sightings in the Southwest correspond with the comings and goings of secret aircraft. Some of the most intense UFO spottings coincided with the testing of the F-117A stealth fighter, which was stationed just west of Area 51. These may account for the yet unexplained sightings.

What better way to hide extraordinary aircraft than to wrap them in the compelling fiction of aliens?

The Media Irresponsibly Encourage Belief in UFOs

Art Levine

Why do so many people believe in questionable UFO "facts," even when the evidence for them is flimsy? Art Levine, a contributing editor for *U.S. News & World Report,* says that the media is responsible. It is so concerned with presenting a "balanced" view that it gives the same amount of credence to both well-informed and weak perspectives. In the following article, Levine comments on the unreasonably balanced news coverage of the fiftieth anniversary of an alleged UFO crash at Roswell, New Mexico.

It's a truism that journalists need to offer a balanced view of all sides when writing about a public controversy. Sometimes, though, one side of a debate consists of sheer hooey, and the press's failure to make this plain does society a disservice. A case in point is the preposterously "objective" coverage of the supposed UFO crash in Roswell, N.M.

A decent case could be made that the Roswell incident's 50th anniversary, which was celebrated [in July 1997], didn't rate much coverage at all, given that the UFO event in question never happened. But *Time's* cover asked, "What *really* happened out there?" as if the answer were somehow in doubt. On CNN and MSNBC, it seemed like all-Roswell, all the time, with no fewer than five live remotes on the anniversary of what CNN called "the UFO sighting" there. There were also in-depth discussions of Roswell that day on two CNN talk shows, *CNN & Co.* and *Talkback Live.*

The weaknesses of "balanced reporting" in this story are illustrated by *USA Today's* coverage of an Air Force report stating that the Roswell "aliens" said to have been glimpsed in 1947 were really crash-test dummies sighted in the mid-1950s. The newspaper said the Air Force "tried to dispel" the flying saucer accounts but, for the sake of balance the paper noted that believers in the Roswell sighting say "key witnesses" wouldn't confuse events in the 1950s with their "vivid recollections" of 1947. "Witnesses include Frank Kaufmann, now 81, who was a civilian employee at the Roswell base and says he saw two of five dead aliens at the crash," the paper said. It quoted Kaufmann: "'They were very good-looking people, ash-colored faces . . . about 5 feet 5 tall, eyes a little more pronounced.'"

Plain folk vs. Big Government: Whom are readers going to believe? A *Time*/Yankelovich poll showed that 65 percent of people think a UFO crashed at Roswell.

A better approach to covering the Roswell story would be to focus on mounting evidence collected by more discriminating UFO researchers that many key Roswell witnesses, in the words of Kal Korff, "aren't telling the truth." Korff is the author of *The Roswell UFO Crash: What They Don't Want You to Know.* He says the media are "treating these witnesses with kid gloves."

Yes, Virginia, many of Roswell's key witnesses have changed their stories several times and have been caught telling falsehoods. Korff's book shows that a first group of eyewitnesses mistakenly believed that some debris from a shattered radar reflector came from a spaceship. These witnesses didn't say anything about alien bodies. After a 1989 TV episode of *Unsolved Mysteries* about Roswell, a second mélange of "witnesses" came forward with bizarre tales of alien sightings. No one in this second group has told a plausible or consistent story. Jim Ragsdale, for one, said he spotted four alien bodies near a spaceship. Later he asserted that he saw nine alien bodies, from which he removed gold helmets, and that he buried the aliens in the sand. Glenn Dennis was, in 1947, a young mortician. He said he was called (or visited) by military officers inquiring about small caskets and later met with a frightened nurse at the base hospital, who drew pictures of bulb-headed aliens for him. Her name was Naomi Selff, he told UFO researchers; she was transferred overseas a few days later and disappeared (or became a nun). Dennis was hailed as "absolutely truthful" by UFO investigator Karl Pflock in a 1994 report. But after learning there was no record of nurse Selff—and no trans- fers of nurses overseas—Pflock now concludes that Dennis didn't tell the truth. Dennis responds, "I may sound like a jerk, but . . . I'm telling the truth." He says he gave a fake name to Pflock to test his ability to keep a secret.

The oddest witness of all is Kaufmann, who claims he's still part of a secret military team that recovered the UFO in 1947—although he was discharged from the military in 1945 and, despite what *USA Today* says, has never substantiated his claim that he later worked at the Roswell base as a civilian. He has told interviewers that everyone from Charles Lindbergh to Werner von Braun was involved in the Roswell incident. When I spoke to Kaufmann last year for MSNBC, I couldn't believe that this tale-spinning old coot was the leading witness in several books and TV shows. He said of his many critics: "It's up to them to disprove me." Korff and Pflock have done so, but it's time for the rest of the media to follow their lead in examining improbable, high-profile UFO claims. Maybe then they could solve the real mystery behind Roswell: how one town's citizens could have gulled so many supposedly tough-minded journalists into thinking their stories had any credence at all.

I Want Proof

Alan Hale

Many people are skeptical that UFOs really exist. One of the most common objections is that there is no objective, tangible proof. In fact, some skeptics say that unless we actually have a UFO and its occupants to examine and study objectively, we will only have guesses about UFOs, not proof. Others say that by using scientific investigation methods, we should be able to draw reasonable conclusions from the evidence that we do have. In the following article, astronomer Alan Hale describes three basic principles he believes those who insist that UFOs are real must address. Hale does not believe there is sufficient evidence in favor of UFOs.

When I am confronted with beliefs about UFOs or other paranormal phenomena—or, for that matter, just about *anything*—I am guided by three basic principles, to wit:

1) *Extraordinary claims require extraordinary evidence.* The discovery that there are other intelligent beings in the universe—and, as a corollary, that life and intelligence can and

has evolved at locations other than Earth—and that, moreover, these beings are visiting Earth on a semi-regular basis in spacecraft that seem to defy the laws of physics as we now know them, would unquestionably rank as the greatest discovery in the history of science, and most definitely is an extraordinary claim. Therefore, in order for me to accept it, you must produce extraordinary evidence. What might this evidence be? For one thing, the aliens themselves. Not some story where someone says that someone says that someone says that they saw aliens, but the actual physical aliens themselves, where I and other trustworthy and competent scientists and individuals can study and communicate with them. I'd like to examine their spacecraft and learn the physical principles under which it operates. I'd like a ride on that spacecraft. I'd like to see their star charts and see where the aliens come from. I'd like to know the astronomical, physical, chemical, and biological conditions of their home world and solar system, and how they compare with and contrast with ours. If possible, I'd like to visit their home world, and any other worlds that might be within their sphere of influence. In other words, I want the aliens visible front and center, where there can be *no reasonable doubt* as to their existence. Stories about "lights" or "things" in the sky do not impress me, especially when such reports come from people who have no idea of the vast array of natural and man-made phenomena that are visible in the sky if one would only take the time to look.

Burden of Proof

2) *The burden of proof is on the positive.* If you are making an extraordinary claim, the burden is on you to produce the extraordinary evidence to prove that you are correct; the burden is not on me to prove that you are wrong. Furthermore, you must prove your case by providing the direct and com-

pelling evidence for it; you can't prove it by eliminating a few token explanations and then crying, "Well, what else can it be?"

3) *Occam's Razor: If one is confronted with a series of phenomena for which there exists more than one viable explanation, one should choose the simplest explanation which fits all the observed facts.* It is an undeniable fact that many people have seen, or at least claimed to see, objects in the sky and on the ground for which they have no explanation. But it is also an undeniable fact that people can make mistakes about their observations. It is an undeniable fact that reports can come from people who are unaware of the various phenomena that are visible in the sky and from people who are not equipped or trained at making reliable scientific observations. It is an undeniable fact that a person's preconceived notions and expectations can affect his/her observations. It is an undeniable fact that some people will lie and will create hoaxes for any one of various reasons. Taking all these undeniable facts together, the simplest explanation—to me, anyway—for the UFO phenomenon is that every report is either a hoax or is a mistake of some sort. If this explanation is incorrect, then you have to increase the sphere of undeniable facts; and for this, see points 1) and 2) above.

Earth Visits Unlikely

To me, it seems extremely likely that life has started and evolved at other sites throughout the universe, quite possibly in a great number of places. It also seems rather possible that, at some of those sites, evolution has created an intelligent species which has developed technology far in advance of our own and which might be capable of interstellar space flight. Despite the incredible distances between stars, and despite the vast dispersion in evolutionary states that must exist throughout the sphere of races that have achieved some sort of sentience, it is possible—although, to me, extremely unlikely—that one or more of these races has visited Earth within the relatively recent past. Indeed, I would be absolutely ecstatic if any such visits have taken place. No one would be happier than me to meet with and converse with these beings and, I dare say, there are very few people who are better prepared intellectually and emotionally to deal with this prospect if it were to occur. But again, I want the direct evidence for their existence; I want the aliens themselves. I don't want to hear stories about some "thing" that some person somewhere might have seen.

As a lifelong amateur astronomer, as a professional astronomer, as someone who has read countless science fiction stories and scientific essays, I have devoted my life to unraveling the secrets of the universe and to pushing humanity and humanity's knowledge as far into space as I can. (This is my reason for claiming that there are few people in the world who are better prepared than I am to meet with an alien race; if there is any human being who *could* meet with alien beings, it would be someone like me.) At the same time, I suspect there is hardly anyone who watches and studies the sky more than I do, and while I have almost continuously observed the sky for most of my lifetime, I have yet to see a single object for which there was not a prosaic explanation. I *have* seen such diverse phenomena as: fireballs, rocket launches, satellite re-entries, comets, auroras, bright planets, novae, orbiting satellites, ionospheric experiments, high-altitude balloons—all of which have been reported as "UFOs" by uninformed witnesses. If indeed there are alien spacecraft flying around Earth with the frequency with which UFO devotees are claiming, then I must ask how come I have never seen anything remotely resembling such an object, while at the same time I have managed to see all these various other types of phenomena.

In summary, I consider it likely that there are advanced alien races somewhere "out there," and I remain open to the possibility that, unlikely as it may seem, one or more such races could be visiting Earth. But if so, where are they? If they possess the technology capable of traveling interstellar distances, then they are so far ahead of us that there can be no reason for them to be afraid of us. If they wish to hide from us, they could do so easily; if they don't wish to, then they have no need to play games with us and only show themselves to a few unwitting individuals. Let them reveal themselves to humanity at large, to our scientists, and to me.

Epilogue: Analyzing the Evidence

A re UFOs fact or fiction? As the articles in this book show, determining the answer is not easy. The subject of UFOs is filled with conflict and controversy. Ufology (the study of UFOs) is a maze of battling experts and conflicting evidence. Those involved with the subject are passionate about it. You might think that those interested in such a specialized topic would be pleased to work together to solve the great mystery of UFOs. However, this is not always the case. For every expert opinion you find about UFOs, you can find another that contradicts it. For every piece of evidence that seems sound, you can find experts who say it is not. For every expert, you can find another who questions the honesty or credentials of the first. To further complicate matters, hoaxers occasionally report bogus UFO sightings.

Often you may read two or more articles that present very different views of the same topic. How can you tell which article—if either—is telling you the truth? It is sometimes very difficult to decide. That is why it is so important to learn how to read critically, especially when you are reading about controversial topics like the ones in this book.

Reading critically does not mean that you criticize, or say negative things, about an article. It means that you analyze and evaluate what you read. You look for clues to decide if an article is truthful and reasonable. This epilogue will describe a technique for reading critically and will give you practice in analyzing the articles in this book.

The Author

Perhaps the first thing you should consider is the article's author. Do you know anything about him or her? If you do, this can be an important clue to the article's worth. Does the author have any special qualifications for writing about this subject? Is the author a respected writer known for getting the facts right? Has the author personally seen a UFO? Is the author a member of a bizarre cult? The answers to these questions can help you decide if the information in the article is worthwhile.

Hypothetical Reasoning

Whether or not you know anything about the author, you can evaluate an article on its own merits by using hypothetical reasoning. Scientists use hypothetical reasoning to determine if scientific ideas are true. Readers can use hypothetical reasoning to help decide if what they read is fact or fiction. (It is important to recognize that using hypothetical reasoning to analyze an article will not necessarily prove that the author's claims are true. However, if it is done properly, it can determine whether the author has presented a reasonable case in support of his or her claim.)

To use hypothetical reasoning to analyze an article, you will use five steps:

1. State the author's claim (the hypothesis).
2. Gather the author's evidence supporting the claim.
3. Examine the evidence the author uses to support the claim.
4. Consider alternative hypotheses (explanations).
5. Draw a conclusion about the author's claim.

If you have two articles dealing with the same issue (for example, one claims that UFOs are fact and the other claims that they are fiction), you can apply hypothetical reasoning to both articles. Then, by comparing your analyses, you can see which author has made the strongest case.

One thing to keep in mind is that critically reading one or two articles will help you determine whether those articles are fact or fiction. But it will probably not give you a final answer to the big issue involved. With a topic as controversial and complex as UFOs, you will probably have to read many articles and books before you can be confident that you have enough evidence to apply hypothetical reasoning to decide if UFOs are real.

In the following sections, we will use hypothetical reasoning to critically examine some of the articles in this book. You can also practice applying the method to other articles.

1. State the author's claim (the hypothesis).

A hypothesis is a statement that can be tested to determine the likelihood of its truth. To evaluate an article critically, you can start by stating a hypothesis—in this case, a statement of the author's claim. The articles in this book each make one or more claims about UFOs, and each article's title alludes to its main claim. The following table shows the major claim of each article, stated as a hypothesis.

Author	Hypothesis
Kenneth J. Arnold	The author saw flying saucers.
Charles Berlitz and William L. Moore	An aircraft from another planet crashed near Roswell, New Mexico, in July 1947.
Don Berliner et al.	Physical evidence near Trans-en-Provence, France, shows that aircraft from other planets may be real.
Lawrence Fawcett and Barry J. Greenwood	
Michael Hesemann	Eyewitness testimony proves that a UFO was seen near NATO airbases in England in 1975.

Author	Hypothesis
Lynn Picknett	
Edward U. Condon	
James McAndrew	An aircraft from another planet did not crash at Roswell, New Mexico, in July 1947.
Paul Devereux	
Bob Berman	People see the planet Venus and mistake it for aircraft from another planet.
Robert L. Park	What people see are illusions, not UFOs.
Jim Wilson	People see experimental aircraft, not UFOs.
Art Levine	The media irresponsibly encourage the belief in UFOs.
Alan Hale	There is no convincing proof that UFOs are real.

One important thing to remember when you write a hypothesis is that it should be a statement that is clear, specific, and provable. Look at the first hypothesis in the table: The author saw flying saucers. At first glance, this statement might appear clear and specific, but it really is not. What is meant by the term *flying saucer*? Literally, it could mean that the author saw flying crockery. It is better to state the hypothesis specifically, like the second hypothesis in the table: An aircraft from another planet crashed near Roswell, New Mexico, in July 1947. Therefore, let's restate the first hypothesis using more specific language:

Kenneth J. Arnold	The author saw aircraft from another planet flying over the Cascade Mountains in June 1947.

The hypotheses that contain the term *UFO* should also

be made more specific. *UFO* stands for "unidentified flying object," which could be any number of things. Some of these authors are actually claiming that the UFOs they are discussing are aircraft from another planet, so their hypotheses should state that. Other authors are claiming that the objects they are discussing are something unidentified, perhaps from another planet, perhaps not. In these cases, the term *UFO* is probably acceptable. (In this epilogue, the term *UFO* will refer to the mysterious phenomena that many people think are aircraft from another planet.)

Now take a look at the last two hypotheses in the table. They are problematic because they cannot easily be proved or disproved. They both contain words with ambiguous meanings. What would be the standard for proving that the media are irresponsible? Who would decide what evidence is convincing? These hypotheses should be changed to provable statements. Here is a more provable hypothesis stating Art Levine's claim:

Art Levine	The media present unproven informa tion about UFOs as if it were fact.

Read Alan Hale's short article and see if you can restate his claim in a more provable way:

Alan Hale	

Not every author has a provable hypothesis, however. If an article is purely the writer's opinion, you may not be able to state a provable hypothesis.

Also keep in mind that some authors may make several important claims in a single article. To examine the article critically, you will need to state a hypothesis for each important claim.

Hypotheses are not listed for four articles in the long table above. Read the articles and write a clear, specific, and provable statement of the author's main claim for each of these four articles.

Kenneth J. Arnold: "The Flying Saucers Are Real"

2. Gather the author's evidence supporting the claim.

Once you have a hypothesis, you must gather the evidence the author uses to support that hypothesis. The evidence is everything the author uses to prove that his or her claim is true. Sometimes a single sentence is a piece of evidence. At other times the evidence consists of a group of several paragraphs. Let's look at the first article in chapter one to see what kind of evidence Kenneth J. Arnold uses to support his claim that he saw aircraft from another planet. (It should be noted that in his article in this book, he does not actually say that what he saw was aircraft from another planet, but he does use the same evidence to make this claim in other articles and books, including one titled *The Flying Saucer as I Saw It*.) The following list presents some of Arnold's evidence:

1. The first piece of evidence is that Arnold describes what he saw.
2. Arnold says the sky and air were "clear as crystal," so the objects were easy to see, and they clearly were not normal aircraft.
3. The objects had an unusual shape; he "couldn't find their tails."
4. The objects exhibited unusual behavior: Arnold had "never before observed airplanes flying so close to the mountaintop."
5. The objects' size was unusually large.
6. The objects' speed was unusually fast.

7. Arnold says he is "accustomed and familiar with most all objects flying," and these craft were unlike anything he had ever seen.
8. The objects flew like geese in a "diagonal chain-like line."
9. The objects were "saucerlike."

3. Examine the evidence the author uses to support the claim.

An author might use many different kinds of evidence to support his or her claims. It is important to recognize different kinds of evidence and to evaluate whether they support the author's claims. Kenneth J. Arnold uses two main kinds of evidence: eyewitness testimony and statements of fact. We will look at those now and consider other kinds of evidence later.

Eyewitness testimony. (Item 1 on the evidence list above.) Eyewitness testimony is a type of anecdotal evidence, a story or personal account that may or may not be able to be verified. (This contrasts with hard evidence, which is usually physical evidence or something measurable.) Anecdotal evidence is commonly used as proof of UFOs and other unusual phenomena precisely because hard evidence is so difficult to obtain. A UFO sighting is usually a fleeting thing, lasting from a few seconds to several minutes. Usually it is completely unexpected, and most do not leave physical evidence behind. Therefore, anecdotal evidence, especially eyewitness accounts, is often the best evidence available.

Kenneth J. Arnold's whole article is an example of eyewitness testimony. The right eyewitness can provide a great deal of information about an event. However, one thing to keep in mind is that eyewitness reports—of anything, not just UFOs—are notoriously unreliable. Because many UFO incidents happen very quickly, the witness only has a few seconds to take it in. (Arnold says his sighting lasted only about two minutes.) The witness will remember some details and forget others. And the more time that passes between the actual incident and the time the witness writes a report or is interviewed, the more likely it is that his or her memory will have changed some of the details. In Arnold's case, he reported the incident almost immediately, but he wrote the report in this book about three weeks after the incident took place.

You may have seen this common eyewitness exercise enacted on a television program: A group of people is sitting in a classroom listening to a lecture or doing some other classroom activity. Suddenly a stranger bursts onto the scene. The stranger may "rob" one of the witnesses or do something else dramatic. Then the stranger leaves.

A few moments later, the instructor asks the students to tell what they witnessed. Invariably, different students remember different things. One remembers that the stranger was of average height and weight; another remembers that he was thin or heavy. One remembers that he had red hair; another remembers that a hood covered his head. One remembers that he was carrying a weapon; another remembers that his hands were empty. And so on. When something unexpected happens, especially when it happens quickly or when it evinces great emotion, the mind is not prepared to remember details. This is why independent corroborating witnesses—witnesses who remember the same thing and who have not discussed it with each other—can be so important in an investigation. Although it is not mentioned in Arnold's article, two or three other people also reported seeing strange objects in the sky at about the same time and place that he did.

People in certain occupations are trained to observe events very meticulously, and they are assumed to be better eyewitnesses than the average person. Pilots fit into this classification, as do police officers. The fact that Arnold was an experienced pilot gives his report some credibility, and Arnold tells us that the sky and air were "clear as crystal" (item 2 on the evidence list) so the objects were easy to see. Pilots often have to make quick, accurate judgments of distance and size, so we can expect that Arnold's estimate of the objects' size and speed (items 5 and 6 on the evidence list) should be more accurate than the average person's. In addition, he was familiar with the appearance of most aircraft known to be flying in 1947.

Another factor in evaluating eyewitness articles is the witness's reputation. Does the witness (Arnold, in this case) have a reputation for honesty? publicity-seeking? exaggeration? scholarship? flakiness? The introduction to Kenneth J. Arnold's article tells you that Arnold was known for his good character and his knowledge about aircraft. It also tells you that the FBI officer who evaluated Arnold's report believed that Arnold was telling the truth about what he saw. (We have to note here that just because the witness is telling the truth does not mean that he saw what he thinks he saw. See the article in this book by Robert L. Park, for example. It is easy for the eye to be fooled and for our perceptions to be influenced by what we expect to see.)

Bias must also be eliminated when evaluating an eyewitness report. *Bias* refers to preconceived ideas about something. In other words, an eyewitness report can be affected by the witness's past experience, by other things he or she knows, by personal prejudice, and other factors. For example, at various times there have been "UFO flaps," when many UFOs were observed by many witnesses over a period of several days, weeks, or even months. When a UFO flap receives newspaper and television coverage, or after a highly publicized movie or television program about UFOs has come out, many more people than normal report seeing

UFOs. Often, these sightings are easily shown to be something else, but the observers are primed to see UFOs, so they interpret any unusual light as a UFO. At the time Kenneth J. Arnold witnessed the "saucerlike objects" over the Cascade Mountains, UFOs were not a common phenomena, so he probably was not influenced by this kind of bias.

Another factor affecting eyewitness reports, especially relating to topics like UFOs, is that sometimes investigators try to help witnesses remember details by using hypnosis. However, many experts consider information gained under hypnosis to be suspect. There is much concern in UFO circles that testimony gained through hypnosis might be influenced by the hypnotist or other factors.

What do you think? Considering the information in this section, does Kenneth J. Arnold appear to be a good eyewitness? Does his eyewitness report support the claim that he saw aircraft from another planet?

Statements of fact. A statement of fact presents information as being true. "Kenneth J. Arnold was a pilot" is a statement of fact. It is stated as a truth, and it can be verified. Beware of statements that look like facts but cannot be confirmed: "Kenneth J. Arnold saw nine aircraft from another planet" is stated as though it were a fact, but we do not know for sure that it is true.

Ideally, to significantly support an author's claims, the statements of fact that he or she uses should be verifiable. They should be something you can look up in an encyclopedia or other reference book. Or the author should tell you the source of the information so that you can confirm it. Or the statements of fact should be something you can test to find out if they are true. However, many authors expect you to accept their statements of fact as true just because they tell you so. Be careful about accepting facts just because the author states them. Look for corroborating evidence (evidence that helps confirm their truth).

Items 3, 4, 5, 6, 7, 8, and 9 on the evidence list are presented as facts. If we accept that Kenneth J. Arnold is a reliable observer, we can probably accept that items 3, 4, 7, 8, and 9 are true. In order to accept items 5 and 6 as facts, we have to believe that Arnold had the ability to accurately estimate these things.

Which of Arnold's statements of fact can be verified, and which cannot?

Now we must consider whether Arnold's statements of fact support the hypothesis that he saw aircraft from another planet. What do you think?

4. Consider alternative hypotheses (explanations).

An important step in critically examining an article is to consider whether the author considers other explanations that might fit his or her facts. If the author considers only one explanation, that might mean that he or she is presenting a biased, or one-sided, view or that he or she has not fully considered the issue.

In his article "I Want Proof," Alan Hale mentions Occam's Razor, the famous principle for considering claims of the unusual. The principle states that the simplest explanation is probably the best. In other words, if the evidence can be explained by something ordinary, there is no reason to look for unusual or exotic explanations. Thus, the critical reader has to determine whether the author has considered other explanations and if he or she has looked for common explanations that will fit the evidence as well as an exotic explanation does.

In the case of UFOs, common explanations that should be examined include weather, astronomical, and aeronautical phenomena. For example, a type of cloud called lenticular resembles UFOs. Certain kinds of moisture or heat con-

ditions can cause reflections resembling lights with no visible source. Fog can make airplane lights look like mysterious disembodied lights. Certain stars and planets appear
brighter at different times of year. A satellite could be mistaken for a UFO.

Something that would explain the illusion of a UFO
should not be overlooked either. For example, if telephone
wires run through the area, a wire weight or a burst balloon
hanging from the wire might look like a flying object at
night when the wires are less visible.

As it happens, Kenneth J. Arnold does consider several
common explanations—jet planes, a reflection or mirage,
rockets and artillery shells—but he rejects them. On page
26 he says, "I assumed they were some type of jet planes,"
but his discoveries about the objects' shape, size, and speed
made him question this explanation. On page 28 he says
that some reporters suggested he might have seen reflections or a mirage, but he states, "This I know to be absolutely false" because he observed the objects from different angles and both through the plane's glass windshield
and through plain air. On page 29 he indicates that he considered rockets and artillery shells but that the objects did
not move in the same way that rockets or artillery shells
would. Do Arnold's rejections of these ordinary explanations seem reasonable to you?

As a critical reader, you should consider information that
is not in the author's article as well. For example, look again
at item 9 on the evidence list and consider: Just because
something looks "saucerlike," does that mean it actually has
a saucer shape? Might the angles and distance from which
Arnold saw the objects and the amount of sunlight and
shadow that played on them make the objects look like
saucers? A writer named James Easton suggests that this is
the case. He points to the "facts" in items 8 and 9 and says

that Arnold may have seen American white pelicans instead of UFOs. Light could flash off pelican wings, and Arnold may have misjudged the distance of the objects, thereby estimating their size and speed wrong. Reviewing the information in the Arnold article, do you think this explanation sounds more plausible than flying saucers?

5. Draw a conclusion about the author's claim.

Finally, after considering the evidence and alternative explanations, it is time to make a judgment, to decide if the hypothesis makes sense. You can tally up the evidence that does and does not support Arnold's claim and see how many pros and how many cons you have. But that is really too simple. You will have to give more weight to some kinds of evidence than to others. For example, almost all of Arnold's evidence is based on his own observation, which may be entirely accurate, but it cannot be verified by any objective means. What do you think—does Kenneth J. Arnold adequately support his claim that he saw aircraft from another planet?

Bob Berman: "Explanation: Venus"

Let's examine another article using hypothetical reasoning. Read Bob Berman's article that begins on page 106.

1. State a hypothesis.

People see the planet Venus and mistake it for aircraft from another planet.

2. Gather the author's evidence.
   1. President Jimmy Carter mistook Venus for a UFO. So did a squadron of World War II fighters flying a mission over Japan.
   2. A survey names Venus sightings as the most common cause of UFO reports.

3. Venus emits intense, concentrated light and remains visible long after twilight.

4. The author's neighborhood probably has more UFO reports than most, made by his "flashback-prone Woodstock region" neighbors.

5. The author prefers to believe that those who "know the sky" do not see UFOs.

6. The author flies airplanes.

7. The author has been watching the skies for forty years and has never seen a UFO.

8. Few knowledgeable amateur astronomers report seeing UFOs.

9. If aliens have the advanced technology that would enable them to covertly travel all the way to Earth, it is unlikely that they would allow themselves to be witnessed.

10. UFOs are never filmed on clear, focused videotape.

11. Some UFO sightings are known to be caused by pranks and hoaxes, so many others may be also.

3. Examine the evidence.

Bob Berman's article is obviously a lighthearted look at what he views as the folly of UFO belief. It is not intended to be a deeply serious examination of the UFO issue. However, it presents a clear claim about the source of most UFO sightings. Berman includes several kinds of evidence in his article, many of them different from the kinds of evidence Kenneth J. Arnold uses. Berman's evidence includes generalizations, statements of fact, ridicule and name-calling, and personal opinion or bias.

Generalizations. (Items 1, 7, 8, 10, and 11 on the evidence list.) A generalization is a broad conclusion based on a few examples. For instance, you might make the generalization "Beach vacations are great!" But in truth, beach vacations are good sometimes and not so good others, depending on the weather, your traveling companions, whether you sunburn easily, and other factors. Or you might visit a friend's house one day and see three people walking their dachshunds. You might generalize that the people in this neighborhood only have dachshunds for pets. But if you were there at another time of day you might discover people walking their poodles, black labs, or other dogs. One visit is probably not sufficient to make a generalization about the kind of dogs in the neighborhood. Although generalizations can be true, they can also be based on inadequate evidence and be false.

Sometimes an author makes an implied generalization. That is, the author names one or two examples and wants the reader to generalize. Bob Berman uses this technique—the implied generalization—several times. In item 1, for example, the author presents two examples of famous "UFO sightings" that turned out to be the planet Venus. The author wants you to generalize that other sightings are probably Venus, too.

In item 7 the author concludes that because he has not seen a UFO, neither has anybody else. One person—himself—is a very small sample on which to base a generalization!

Generalizations are sometimes true, but without sufficient evidence to back them up, they do not prove much. Be aware of what evidence lies behind a generalization.

Look at items 10 and 11. What is the author's implied generalization? Decide if it is justified.

Statements of fact. (Items 2, 3, 6, and 10 on the evidence list.) Review the section about statements of fact in the section of this epilogue that discusses Kenneth J. Arnold's article. Then look at items 2, 3, 6, and 10 and decide whether they are good evidence for Bob Berman's hypothesis.

Ridicule and name-calling. (Items 4 and 9 on the evidence list.) Ridicule and name-calling are popular methods of showing that those who do not agree with you are wrong. They are not evidence for the author's hypothesis. Instead, they cast doubt on the author's opponents. "Flashback-prone Woodstock region" is a reference to the "psychedelic era" of the 1960s and 1970s when a segment of the young population was known to take hallucinogenic drugs and to have hallucinatory flashbacks long after using the substances. The author is suggesting that his neighbors were alive during that era, so any UFOs they report are probably hallucinations. The author is writing humorously, but at the same time he is ridiculing the idea of UFO sightings. He wants the reader to conclude that seeing UFOs is a ridiculous idea.

In item 9 he is also using ridicule to dismiss serious consideration of UFOs.

Personal opinion or bias. (Item 5 on the evidence list.) Many authors try to hide their bias about their subject, but Berman states it clearly in item 5.

4. Consider alternative hypotheses.

Does Bob Berman consider alternative hypotheses? He does consider hoaxes as another explanation for UFO sightings. Can you think of other hypotheses he should examine?

5. Draw a conclusion.

You decide: Does Bob Berman make a good case for Venus being the explanation for most UFO sightings? What evidence most influences your decision?

Other Kinds of Evidence

Here are some additional types of evidence authors commonly use to support their claims.

Celebrity or expert testimonial. Many writers support their claims with testimony from a celebrity or an expert. A lot of television ads do this. You have probably seen the GAP commercials that have popular entertainers singing while wearing GAP jeans, and you have seen commercials for aspirin and other medicines that have a doctor praising the medicine. Advertisers know that many people are influenced when a celebrity or an expert says something is true.

Celebrity testimony usually does not have much value as evidence: If a celebrity wears a certain brand of jeans, does it mean the jeans are good quality? If an automobile commercial shows a famous architect looking at a car and saying that he likes to look at beautiful things, does that mean the car is a well-built, reliable vechicle?

Expert testimony can provide valuable evidence, however. In the case of physical traces left by UFOs, for example, experts in chemistry, biology, and mineralogy can provide valuable information about burn marks, damaged foliage, and metals. The expert does need to be an expert on the topic being considered, however. A biology expert cannot necessarily provide important information about metal composition.

An author who uses expert testimony should provide sufficient information for readers to judge whether that person is qualified on the topic. Jim Wilson, author of "Explanation: Experimental Aircraft," quotes an expert in his second paragraph. The subject is what the CIA knows about UFOs. Wilson identifies his expert, Gerald K. Haines, this way: "A historian for the National Reconnaissance Office who studied secret CIA UFO files for an internal CIA study that examined the spy agency's involvement in UFOs through the 1990s." This description clearly tells the reader that Haines qualifies as an expert in this area.

Statistical evidence. Authors sometimes use statistics or other numerical data to support their claims. For example, they may cite a survey or state that a certain percentage of people have observed mysterious lights. Be sure to carefully evaluate numerical claims. Just because a large number of people claim to have seen mysterious lights does not prove that they saw aircraft from another planet. Also pay attention to where the author obtained the information. In Bob Berman's article, analyzed above, item 2 mentions a survey the author uses to support his hypothesis that people who think they see UFOs are really seeing the planet Venus. In this case, Berman does not provide any information about the survey, so this information is not very helpful. But if he had cited statistics from the survey, you would need to know more about the survey in order to determine whether the statistics really supported his claim.

When anlyzing statistical evidence, consider the following: When was the survey conducted? (Was it in 1919? 1950? 1999? Our knowledge of UFOs and Venus has changed over the years, and the answers would reflect the knowledge of the time.) Who conducted it? (Was it an independent polling organization such as the Gallup Group? Was it UFO buffs? Astronomy buffs? Each group would have its own biases that could influence the survey.) How many people were surveyed, and who were they? (It makes quite a difference whether a dozen people or a thousand were surveyed! And it makes a lot of difference if the people were astronomers or members of a UFO club, volunteers or part of a scientifically selected group. Volunteers tend to have a particular interest in the topic being studied, so their views may not be typical of the general population. Professional pollsters know how to select participants so that they represent a true cross-section of the population, representing people of different ages, races, educational backgrounds, and so on.) The survey's questions and the way they are phrased can also affect the survey's results.

Logical fallacy. Logic comes from the Greek word for reason. *Logical thinking* means to reason things out. (Hypothetical reasoning is a form of logical reasoning.) A logical fallacy is when logical reasoning fails. You think you are reasoning logically, but you are not.

A generalization can be an example of logical fallacy: "I have never seen a UFO, therefore, UFOs do not exist."

Another type of logical fallacy makes a false analogy. That is, it wrongly compares two items based on a common quality. Here is an example:

Honey bees make honey. Honey bees have yellow stripes.
Wasps also have yellow stripes, so wasps must make honey.

The fallacy is that yellow stripes have nothing to do with the ability to make honey, so the argument falls apart.

Here's another example:

The witness saw a saucer-shaped craft flying in the sky.
UFOs are saucer-shaped, so the witness must have seen a UFO.

This fallacy is twofold: First, lots of things are shaped like saucers (Frisbees, pie pans, saucers, and some kites) and others could look like saucers under certain conditions. Second, no one knows for sure what UFOs—if they do exist— look like; witnesses have reported many different shapes, including saucer, bullet, and triangle.

Physical evidence. In some UFO cases, there is physical evidence that can be studied. This might include burned or deformed grass or other vegetation, indentations in the ground, or odd substances such as pieces of strange metal. If an article describes physical evidence, it should tell how the evidence was investigated. Generally, a qualified investigator (someone who knows how to collect evidence without contaminating it) will photograph the evidence in place and then take samples to be analyzed in a lab—or, preferably, in two or more independent laboratories.

Depending on the type of evidence, a laboratory can analyze it for chemical makeup, cell damage or mutation, magnetism, radiation, and various other things. The aim will be to discover if there is anything unusual about the sample or if, for example, the metal is typical of that used in farm machinery or if burnt grass is the same as any grass burned with matches or gasoline.

Sometimes a witness is affected physically. Some UFO witnesses have received strange burns or other marks. A credible author will explain how these were examined to rule out common explanations and determine their possible causes.

In some lucky cases, a UFO witness is able to take a photo or a video of the UFO. In fact, there is a history of stunning and convincing UFO photos dating back to the time of Project Blue Book. In recent years, amazing videos have shown up in UFO circles and on television programs.

The challenge is proving that the film is undoctored and that it does not simply show something normal in an unusual light. This challenge has become ever greater as technology has become more and more sophisticated and inexpensive. A couple of decades ago, if you had the original negative, a doctored film was fairly easy to discover. A really good fake could only be made with rare and expensive photographic equipment. Today, with computers and digital cameras readily available, it has become fairly easy for people without special skills to make a fake UFO photo or video, and some of these are extremely difficult to detect without the help of real experts with sophisticated equipment.

Read the article "Evidence: Physical Traces in France" by Don Berliner and others. Do the authors tell how the evidence was examined? How it was analyzed and by whom? Were the analyzers experts qualified to do this kind of analysis? Does the physical evidence described in this article prove that UFOs exist? Explain.

Now You Do It!

Choose one article from this book that has not already been analyzed and use hypothetical reasoning to determine if the author's evidence supports the hypothesis. Here is a form you can use:

Name of article_____ Author_____

1. State the author's hypothesis.

2. List the evidence.

3. Examine the evidence. For each item listed under number 2, state what type of evidence it is (eyewitness testimony, statement of fact, etc.) and evaluate it: Does it appear to be valid evidence? Does it appear to support the author's hypothesis?

4. Consider alternative hypotheses. (What alternative explanations does the author consider? Does he or she examine them fairly? If the author rejects them, does the rejection seem reasonable? Are there other alternative explanations you believe should be considered? Explain.)

5. Draw a conclusion about the hypothesis. Does the author adequately support his or her claim? Do you believe the author's hypothesis holds up under scrutiny? Explain.

For Further Research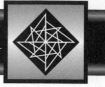

Robert E. Bartholomew, "Before Roswell: The Meaning Behind the Crashed-UFO Myth," *Skeptical Inquirer,* May/June 1998.

Don Berliner with Marie Galbraith and Antonio Huneeus, *UFO Briefing Document: The Best Available Evidence.* New York: Dell, 2000.

Charles Berlitz and William L. Moore, *The Roswell Incident: The Classic Study of UFO Contact.* New York: Grosset & Dunlap, 1980.

Bob Berman, "Strange Universe," *Astronomy,* March 2001.

Peter Brookesmith, *UFO: The Government Files.* New York: Barnes and Noble, 1996.

Jerome Clark, *The UFO Book: Encyclopedia of the Extraterrestrial.* Detroit: Visible Ink Press/Gale Research, 1998.

———, *The UFO Encyclopedia,* 3 vols. 2nd rev. ed. Detroit: Omnigraphics Press/Gale Research, 1997.

Edward U. Condon, *Final Report of the Scientific Study of Unidentified Flying Objects.* New York: E.P. Dutton, 1969.

Paul Devereux, *Earth Lights Revelation: UFOs and Mystery Lightform Phenomena: The Earth's Secret Energy Force.* London: Blandford, 1989.

Ann Druffel, "Magnetic Anomalies and UFO Flight," *Mufon UFO Journal,* Part I: May 1980; Part II: June 1980.

Hilary Evans and Dennis Stacy, eds., *Fortean Times Presents UFO 1947–1997: Fifty Years of Flying Saucers.* London: John Brown, 1997.

Lawrence Fawcett and Barry J. Greenwood, *The UFO Cover-Up: What the Government Won't Say.* New York: Prentice-Hall, 1984.

"50 Years of UFOs," *FATE,* June 1997.

Cynthia Fox, "The Search for Extraterrestrials: Why on Earth Do We Still Believe?" *Life,* March 1, 2000.

Kendrick Frazier, Barry Karr, and Joe Nickell, *The UFO Invasion.* Amherst, NY: Prometheus Books, 1997.

Bernard D. Gildenberg and David E. Thomas, "Case Closed: Reflections on the 1997 Air Force Roswell Report," *Skeptical Inquirer,* May/June 1998.

Craig Glenday, *The UFO Investigator's Handbook.* Philadelphia: Running Press, 1999.

Timothy Good, *Above Top Secret: The Worldwide UFO Cover-Up.* New York: Quill/William Morrow, 1988.

Jeff Greenwald, "Who's Out There?" *Discover,* April 1999.

Alan Hale, "An Astronomer's Personal Statement on UFOs," *Skeptical Inquirer,* March/April 1997

Richard Hall, *The UFO Evidence.* New York: Barnes and Noble, 1997.

———, *The UFO Evidence, Vol. II: A Thirty-Year Report.* Lanham, MD: Scarecrow Press, 2001.

Headquarters United States Air Force, *The Roswell Report: Fact versus Fiction in the New Mexico Desert.* Washington, DC: U.S. Government Printing Office, 1995.

Allan Hendry, *The UFO Handbook: A Guide to Investigating, Evaluating, and Reporting UFO Sightings.* Garden City, NY: Doubleday, 1979.

Michael Hesemann, *UFOs: The Secret History.* New York: Marlowe, 1998.

Antonio Huneeus, "UFO Hoaxes," *FATE*, September 1994.

J. Allen Hynek, "Are Flying Saucers Real?" *Saturday Evening Post*, Part I: December 10, 1966; Part II: December 17, 1966.

——, *The UFO Experience: A Scientific Inquiry*. Chicago: Henry Regnery, 1972.

Leon Jaroff, "Did Aliens Really Land?" *Time*, June 23, 1997.

John A. Keel, *UFOs: Operation Trojan Horse*. New York: G.P. Putnam's Sons, 1976.

Philip J. Klass, *UFOs: The Public Deceived*. Buffalo, NY: Prometheus Press, 1983.

Kal Korff, *The Roswell UFO Crash: What They Don't Want You to Know*. New York: Dell, 2000.

Martin Kottmeyer, "UFO Flaps: An Analysis," *Anomalist*, Winter 1995–1996.

Lynne Lamberg, "Belief in Alien UFOs Deep in American Psyche," *Journal of the American Medical Association*, July 16, 1997.

Bruce Maccabee, *UFO-FBI Connection: The Secret History of the Government's Cover-Up*. St. Paul, MN: Llewellyn, 2000.

James McAndrew, *The Roswell Report: Case Closed*. Washington, DC: U.S. Goverment Printing Office, 1997.

Susan McClelland and John Betts, "UFOs—Is There a Middle Ground Between Skepticism and Belief?" *MacLean's*, August 13, 2001.

Robert L. Park, "Welcome to Planet Earth," *The Sciences*, May 2000.

Curtis Peebles, *Watch the Skies! A Chronicle of the Flying Saucer Myth.* Washington, DC: Smithsonian Institution Press, 1994.

Lynn Picknett, *The Mammoth Book of UFOs.* New York: Carroll and Graf, 2001.

Kevin D. Randle, *Scientific Ufology: Roswell and Beyond—How Scientific Methodology Can Prove the Reality of UFOs.* New York: HarperTorch, 1999.

Jenny Randles, *From Out of the Blue: The Facts in the UFO Cover-Up at Bentwaters NATO Air Base.* New York: Berkley, 1993.

Robert Schaeffer, "The Truth Is, They Never Were Saucers," *Skeptical Inquirer,* September/October 1997.

Dennis Stacy, "UFOs: Going Around in Circles? If Flying Saucers Don't Exist, Why Do So Many People Keep Seeing Them?" *Omni,* September/October 1992.

Dennis Stacy and Patrick Huyghe, "Cosmic Conspiracy: Six Decades of Government UFO Cover-Ups," in six parts: *Omni,* April 1994; May 1994; June 1994; July 1994; August 1994; September 1994.

Ronald D. Story, ed., *The Encyclopedia of Extraterrestrial Encounters.* New York: New American Library, 2001.

Jacques Vallee, *Dimensions: A Casebook of Alien Contact.* New York: Ballantine, 1988.

Erich von Däniken, *Chariots of the Gods?* New York: Bantam, 1968.

Larry Warren and Peter Robbins, *Left at Eastgate.* New York: Marlowe, 1997.

Jim Wilson, "When UFOs Landed," *Popular Mechanics,* May 2001.

Index

Above Top Secrecy: The Worldwide UFO Cover-Up (Good), 18

Air Force, U.S.
  exercises in misinformation by, 67–68
  hypothesis of, 133
  investigations of UFOs by first, 9–11
  "heroic period" of, 10
  report on 1947 New Mexico sightings, 83–94
  public confidence in, 20

Altschuler, Martin D., 97

Alvarez, Luis, 69

Amarante case, 43, 44

analysis. *See* critical reading/analysis

Anderson, Gerald, 85

Area 51, 19

Arnold, Kenneth J., 8–9, 23
  critical evaluation of, 136–43
  hypothesis of, 133

A12 spyplane, 119–20

balloons. *See* research balloons

Berliner, Don, 38
  critical evaluation of, 150

Berlitz, Charles, 30, 82
  hypothesis of, 133

Berman, Bob, 106
  critical evaluation of, 143–46, 148
  hypothesis of, 133

Bible, the, 7

Bounais, Michel, 42

Brown, Frank M., 24

Burquette, William C., 24

Burroughs, John, 61

Bustinza, Adrian, 58, 61

Butler, Brenda, 56–58

Carter, Jimmy, 106

Center for Physical Trace Research, 21

Central Intelligence Agency (CIA), 69
  concerns over UFOs by, 70–71
  cover-up of UFO data by, 71–73
  deception by, 118–19

Cernan, Eugene, 7–8

Christelle case, 43, 44

Citizens Against UFO Secrecy (CAUS), 46–47, 68

Condon, Edward U., 11, 75

Condon Committee, 10, 11, 18

Conrad, Ted, 59

Crickmore, Paul F., 119, 120

critical reading/analysis, 131
  author credibility and, 132
  hypothetical reasoning and, 132–36
  importance of, 80

crop circles, 15

Defense Intelligence Agency (DIA), 48, 51

Dennis, Glenn, 124
Devereux, Paul, 95, 96
  hypothesis of, 133
Dulles, Allen W., 71, 119

earthlights
  as explanation for UFOs,
    95–105
  witness of, and tectonic
    strain, 102
earthquakes
  association with earthlights,
    98–102
Easton, James, 142
Estes, Russ, 13
extraterrestrials
  anthropomorphic dummies
    as explanation for, 87–90
  belief in, 8
  human abductions by,
    explanations for, 113–15
eyewitness testimony. See
  testimony, eyewitness
Ezekiel, 7

Fawcett, Lawrence, 19, 46,
  59–60, 62
  hypothesis of, 133
Fieldguide to UFOs (Stacy and
  Huyghe), 13
Flying Saucer Conspiracy, The
  (Keyhoe), 66
Flying Saucer Review, 97
Flying Saucers Are Real, The
  (Keyhoe), 66
Flying Saucers from Outer Space
  (Keyhoe), 66
Fort, Charles, 100
Fortean events, 100, 101
France-Soir (magazine), 42
Freedom of Information Act
  (1966, 1974), 19, 68
Friedman, Stanton, 31, 82

Galbraith, Marie, 38
Gallup Organization, 8, 20
General Accounting Office, 82
Good, Timothy, 18
Gooding, Barry, 104
government, U.S.
  is hiding UFO information,
    65–73
  con, 79–80
  kept UFO myth alive,
    118–19
  secrecy of, 18–20
  in Roswell case, 66, 68–69
Graham, Richard H., 120
Greenwood, Barry J., 19, 46
  hypothesis of, 133
Groupe d'Etudes des
  Phénomènes Aérospatiaux
  Non-identifiée (GEPAN),
  39, 42

Haines, Gerald K., 118, 147
Hale, Alan, 126, 141
  hypothesis of, 133, 135
Halt, Charles I., 56, 58, 62, 63
Hesemann, Michael, 55
  hypothesis of, 133
Huffer, Charles, 48
Huneeus, Antonio, 17, 38
Huyghe, Patrick, 13
Hynek, J. Allen, 10, 11
hypnosis
  testimony gained under,
    140

Iran Times, 52

Joe Le Taxi case, 43, 44
Journal of Scientific Exploration,
  42

Kaufmann, Frank, 123–24
Kayhan International, 47

Keel, John, 97, 98
Keyhoe, Donald E., 10, 66, 67
Korff, Kal, 124

Lafrenière, Gyslaine F., 100
Lagarde, Ferdinand, 97
Lazarenko, Galina, 98
Leach, Ed, 24
Levine, Art, 122
  hypothesis of, 133, 135
Life (magazine), 20
light effects, 13
Los Angeles Times, 7

machinery
  UFO interference with,
    13–14
Mack, John E., 114
Maltais, Vern, 85
Mantell, Thomas F., Jr., 9
Marcel, Jesse A., 31
McAndrew, James, 81
McDonald, James E., 10
Melnichuk, Alexei, 98
MIJI Quarterly, 53
Mischera, Eric, 59
Moore, Charles B., 91
Moore, William L., 30, 82
  hypothesis of, 133

National Aeronautics and
  Space Administration
  (NASA)
  instrument testing for, 94
National Center for Space
  Studies (France), 39
National Investigations
  Committee on Aerial
  Phenomenon (NICAP), 67
National UFO Reporting
  Center, 21
Nicolai, Renato, 39
Occam's Razor, 128, 141

Omni (magazine), 59
opinion polls. See surveys

Park, Bill, 120
Park, Robert L., 111
  hypothesis of, 133
Persinger, Michael A., 100, 102
Pflock, Karl, 124
Picknett, Lynn, 65
Popular Mechanics (magazine),
  118
Price, Richard, 114
Pritchard, David E., 114
Project Aquatone, 119
Project Blue Book, 10, 11, 17,
  67
  CIA and debunking of UFO
    data in, 71–72
  final conclusions of, 75–80
Project Grudge, 9, 67
Project MOGUL, 83, 91, 92
Project Sign, 9, 67, 68
pseudoscience
  influence on belief in
    UFOs, 115–16
Purdy, Ken, 66

Ragsdale, James, 85, 124
Ramey, Roger, 81
Randle, Kevin, 13
Randles, Jennie, 58
reasoning, hypothetical
  evaluation of articles and,
    132–36
Report on Unidentified Flying
  Objects (Ruppelt), 72
research balloons
  construction of, 91–94
  as explanation of Roswell
    sightings, 81–94
Robertson, H.P., 69
Robertson Panel, 69–70, 71,
  72

Rockefeller, Laurence, 38
Roswell, New Mexico, case
    explanations for, 111–16
        meteoroids, 112–13
        misperceptions, 112–13
        research balloons, 81–94
    government secrecy
        regarding, 66, 68–69
    the media encourage belief
        in, 122–25
    Robertson Panel and, 70
    Twining memo and, 68–69
    U.S. Air Force report on,
        83–94
    public confidence in, 20
Roswell Incident, The (William
    L. Moore and Berlitz), 30,
    31, 82
Roswell Record, 81
*Roswell UFO Crash: What They
    Don't Want You to Know, The*
    (Korff), 124
Ruppelt, Edward J., 9, 71, 72

Sagan, Carl, 116
Schiff, Steven H., 82
*Scientific Study of Unidentified
    Flying Objects* (Altschuler),
    97
Selff, Naomi, 124
Service d'Expertise des
    Phénomènes de Rentrées
    Atmosphériques (SEPRA),
    39, 45
Shields, Henry, 53, 54
spacecrafts, NASA
    testing of, 94
Spaceships of the Visitors
    (Randle and Estes), 13
*Space-Time Transients and
    Unusual Events* (Persinger
    and Lafrenière), 100
Spaulding, John P., 15

SR-71 Revealed (Graham), 120
SR-71 spyplane, 120–21
Stacy, Dennis, 13
Stealth B-2 bomber, 117
Street, Don, 58
surveys
    on belief in extraterrestrials
        and UFOs, 8
    on belief in Roswell
        incident, 123
    of air force report on, 20
    on government secrecy, 116

Tectonic Strain Theory (TST),
    101–102
tectonic stress, 100–102
testimony
    of celebrities or experts, 147
    eyewitness, 137
        assessment of, 138–39
        bias in, 139–40
        military, of UFOs, in
            England, 55–64
        of Renato Nicolai, 40–41
        of Roswell case, 84–85
Time (magazine), 123
Trans-en-Provence case, 39,
    43, 44–45
    eyewitness report on, 40–41
    physical evidence of, 41–42
Twining, Nathan F., 68
Twining Memo, 68–69

*UFO Cover-Up: What the
    Government Won't Say*
    (Fawcett and Greenwood),
    19
*UFO Experience: A Scientific
    Inquiry, The* (Hynek), 12
ufology, 131
UFO(s)
    are real, 23–29
    burden of proof in, 127–28

classification of, 11–12
crashed near Roswell, New
    Mexico, 30–37
critical evaluation of
    accounts of
        evidence in, 147–48,
            149–50
        generalizations in,
            144–45
        as logical fallacies, 149
        ridicule in, 146
        statement of fact in,
            140–41, 145–46
    evidence of
        in France, 38–45
        is insufficient, 75–80,
            126–30
        radar and visual sighting,
            in Tehran, 46–54
        in Roswell case, 66,
            68–69
        secret, possibility of,
            18–20, 116
    explanations for
        alternative, in critical
            evaluation of articles,
            141–42
        experimental aircraft,
            117–21
        hoaxes, 17, 108
        metaphysical, 17
        meteoroids, 112–13
        misperception, 15–16,
            113
        natural earthlights,
            95–105
        psychological, 16–17
        research balloons, 81–94
        tectonic stress, 100–102
        Venus sightings, 106–10
    meaning of, 8

the media encourage belief
    in, 122–25
sightings of
    common characteristics
        of, 12–14
    in England, 55–64
    fault lines as
        explanation for,
        103–105
    in France, 38–45
    number of, 20
    in Roswell, New Mexico,
        30–37
    in Washington state,
        1947, 25–29
sounds of, 13
strange events associated
    with, 14–15
validity of term, 135
UFOs—Operation Trojan Horse
    (Keel), 97
USA Today, 123

Vallee, Jacques, 17
Vandenburg, Hoyt S., 69
Velasco, Jean-Jacques, 44, 45
Venus
    sightings of, as explanation
        for UFOs, 106–10

Warren, Larry, 59–61
websites, 21
Williams, Gordon, 58, 59
Wilson, Jim, 117, 147
    hypothesis of, 133
witnesses
    effects of tectonic strain on,
        102
Wright-Patterson Air Force
    Base, 9, 19, 67